The Lived Experience of Democracy

Working and Writing for Change

Series Editors: Steve Parks and Jessica Pauszek

The Working and Writing for Change series began during the 100th-anniversary celebrations of NCTE. It was designed to recognize the collective work of teachers of English, Writing, Composition, and Rhetoric to work within and across diverse identities to ensure the field recognizes and respects language, educational, political, and social rights of all students, teachers, and community members. While initially solely focused on the work of NCTE/CCCC Special Interest Groups and Caucuses, the series now includes texts written by individuals in partnership with other communities struggling for social recognition and justice.

Books in the Series

CCCC/NCTE Caucuses

Viva Nuestro Caucus: Rewriting the Forgotten Pages of Our Caucus ed. by Romeo García, Iris D. Ruiz, Anita Hernández & María Paz Carvajal Regidor

History of the Black Caucus National Council Teachers of English by Marianna White Davis

Listening to Our Elders: Working and Writing for Social Change by Samantha Blackmon, Cristina Kirklighter, & Steve Parks

Building a Community, Having a Home: A History of the Conference on College Composition and Communication ed. by Jennifer Sano-Franchini, et al.

Community Publications

Steal the Street: The Intersection of Homelessness and Gentrification by Mark Mussman

Literacy and Pedagogy in an Age of Misinformation and Disinformation ed. by Tara Lockhart, Brenda Glascott, Chris Warnick, Juli Parrish, & Justin Lewis

Faces of Courage: Ten Years of Building Sanctuary by Harvey Finkle

Equality and Justice: An Engaged Generation, a Troubled World by Michael Chehade, Alex Granner, Ahmed Abdelhakim Hachelaf, Madhu Napa, Samantha Owens, & Steve Parks

Other People's English: Code-Meshing, Code-Switching, and African American Literacy by Vershawn Ashanti Young, Rusty Barrett, Y'Shanda Young-Rivera, & Kim Brian Lovejoy

Becoming International: Musings on Studying Abroad in America, ed. by Sadie Shorr-Parks

Dreams and Nightmares: I Fled Alone to the United States When I Was Fourteen by Liliana Velásquez. edited and translated by Mark Lyon

The Weight of My Armor: Creative Nonfiction and Poetry by the Syracuse Veterans' Writing Group, ed. by Ivy Kleinbart, Peter McShane, & Eileen Schell

PHD to PhD: How Education Saved My Life by Elaine Richardson

The Lived Experience of Democracy

CRITICIZING INJUSTICE, BUILDING COMMUNITY

Edited by
Kaitlyn Baker
Sophia Cheng
Elise Ebert
Hannah Ellis
Keilah Gadson
Angela Grey-Theriot
Niharika Singhvi

Parlor Press
Anderson, South Carolina
www.parlorpress.com

Parlor Press LLC, Anderson, South Carolina, USA
Copyright © 2023 by New City Community Press

Library of Congress Cataloging-in-Publication Data on File

1 2 3 4 5

978-1-64317-364-1 (paperback)
978-1-64317-365-8 (PDF)
978-1-64317-366-5 (EPUB)

Working and Writing for Change
An Imprint Series of Parlor Press
Series Editors: Steve Parks and Jessica Pauszek

Book Design: Justin Lewis // justinlewis.me

Parlor Press, LLC is an independent publisher of scholarly and trade titles in print and multimedia formats. This book is available in paper and ebook formats from Parlor Press on the World Wide Web at www.parlorpress.com or through online and brick-and-mortar bookstores. For submission information or to find out about Parlor Press publications, write to Parlor Press, 3015 Brackenberry Drive, Anderson, South Carolina, 29621, or email editor@parlorpress.com.

Acknowledgments

We would first and foremost like to thank Professor Parks for giving us the opportunity to work with him on this rewarding project. His unwavering patience and wisdom We would additionally like to thank all of the students who contributed their time and efforts to create this anthology. Your words, experiences, and efforts have tremendous power and influence. We would like to give our thanks and appreciation to all individuals dedicated to the fight for the improvement and establishment of an equitable and inclusive democracy.

Kaitlyn:
Kaitlyn would like to thank her parents, Lisa and Curtis Baker, and her Pop-pop, Jack King, for their tireless support. She would also like to thank the women who preceded her in academia for their persistence and courage in creating an equal role for women in education

Niharika:
Niharika Singhvi would like to thank her papa and mummy, Nilesh and Sneh, and her bhaiya, Bhaskar, for loving unconditionally, for always steering her in the right direction, and for nurturing a beautiful home that is safe and warm. Niharika would also like to thank her friends for bringing such joy and laughter into her life, and for inspiring her in endless ways.

Angie:
Angela Grey-Theriot would like to give a special thank you to her family; especially her parents Cecilia and John Grey-Theriot, for their unconditional support and love and her sisters Francine and Michelle Grey-Theriot, whose constant teasing has brought much needed laughter into her life .

Sophia:
Sophia Cheng would especially like to thank her parents, Chun Ma and Hao Cheng, for their unwavering support and encouragement; her sister, Anna Cheng, for being a source of positive energy; her grandparents, Mingjun

Wang and Chengzuo Ma, for their kind words and warm meals; and her cats, Tiger and Daisy, for providing endless cuddles and companionship.

Keilah:
Keilah Gadson would like to thank her wonderful family, her mother Dee, grandmother and grandfather, Nanny and Gene, and her aunt and uncle, TT and Kevin for always being a source of inspiration, love, and warmth. Furthermore, she would like to thank the friends who have always been like a second family to her, for their decision to stand beside her and love her unconditionally.

Hannah:
Hannah Ellis would like to thank her parents, Scott and Kimberly Ellis, as well as her sisters, Kristen and Lauren Ellis, for their encouragement and love. She would also like to thank her mentor and friend Mr. Moseley for his selfless and lighthearted guidance in and beyond the classroom.

CONTENTS

Introduction

Kaitlyn Baker, Sophia Cheng, Elise Ebert, Hannah Ellis,
Keilah Gadson, Angela Grey-Theriot, Niharika Singhvi

The Lived Experience of Democracy: Criticizing Injustice, Building Community reflects the exploratory efforts of students attempting to make sense of their surroundings. We are a group of students who have been living and working within a university that bears the marks of centuries of racism and exclusion. As students at the University of Virginia, we regularly walk along the infamous Serpentine Walls that once hid the labor of enslaved peoples from the earliest students at the University. We walk within a history that echoes with the racist and sexist admission process of the university that denied admission to Black students until 1950 and admission to women students until 1970. And through much of this history, student activists have been fighting for recognition of those people hidden behind those walls and those people excluded from attending. These students coupled their educational goals with the goal of moving the University to-wards accountability and equity. Resistance, however, has often been fierce. The powerful work of student advocacy groups on grounds has been continually met by individuals and coalitions who wish to suppress democratic practices, inclusive values. Many of the authors in this anthology watched as white supremacists invaded the campus just four years ago, leading to the murder of a young woman, Heather Heyer. The "Unite the Right" rally was a sign to all of us at the Univer-sity of Virginia, as well as many others nationally, to take on a more active role in reforming the current state of our democracy.

Yet students continue to push forward. *The Minority Rights Coalition* (MRC) was instrumental in calling for the removal of Confederate statues on grounds and for increased investment in Black students and faculty. In their "March to Reclaim Grounds," the MRC began the process of healing our university community after the violence of the August rally. UnDocUVA, a group which advocates for the needs of undocumented students on this campus and others, was critical in convincing the administration to allow all students, regardless of their immigration and citizenship status, to enroll at this University. And together, the Black Student Alliance and UnDocUVA provide for the material needs of matriculating students, organizing mutual aid and education programs. Such groups tirelessly petition the university to make good on the promises of democracy. In the case of the Black Student Alliance, students have been reiterating similar demands since the group was founded in 1969. The successes of these groups are due to both the passion of the collective and the skill of the individual. Every group requires dedicated individuals that are willing to take on the work of engaging with democracy. This anthology will include narratives written by such dedicated individuals working collectively and seeking to critically engage and create a more just future.

Despite a resurgence in neo-Nazi and supremacists, we would also argue our generation has not faltered. Over the years, we have witnessed significant and alarming political events. In January of 2021, white supremacists invaded a primary symbol of democracy—the Capitol building. Yet, six months later, the statue of Robert E. Lee, which had provoked a white supremacist march on "the grounds," fell after the dedicated efforts of Charlottesville High School students and community leaders. The mob at the Capitol failed to overthrow American democratic processes, just as the mob at the "Unite the Right " rally failed to stem the power of careful and continuous efforts towards progress. We are not naïve, however. We recognize these alarming events convey the necessity of protecting this democracy, and this anthology makes a case for youth involvement in those efforts. The generation responsible for the creation of this anthology has been involved in efforts for gun safety, racial justice, reproductive rights and justice, LGBTQ+ rights, and the constant interrogation of unjust social systems. Their actions represent the youth asserting their control over their spaces and claiming their responsibilities to petition leadership for justice. And our aim as editors is to demonstrate that if our democracy is threatened, the youth must play (and have been playing) a significant role in breaking down and reconstructing the political narrative to promote justice. We created this anthology by building off of the traditions of free speech and intellectual inquiry on a college campus as an appeal to the public to listen to our voices and experiences.

Here we want to make an important point about young adults asserting control over the spaces they inhabit: This anthology is not only *composed* of essays by student writers, but also *edited* by students. As an editorial collective, worked collaboratively to review and then select what would appear in this anthology and, in doing so, hoped to have demonstrated the ability of students to interrupt and transform who produces knowledge within a university and whose voices are considered "intellectual." This book is therefore important not only for our generation of students at UVA, but for those future generations as an example of how the power and conviction of their voices can shift whose knowledge, whose values, will shape the educational and political future. And in response to a media echo chamber that too often portrays a negative and naive depiction of our generation (Gen Z), we wanted this anthology to demonstrate that our generation has answers, solutions, and opinions on the way *we* want the world to look. For this reason, we selected essays that explore a variety of different perspectives, essays that use research and personal experience, to analyze the current cultural and political environment.

And here, we would argue an anthology is a beautiful vessel to achieve these goals. An anthology is one of the only ways a single work can make space for such a diversity of opinions, experiences, and ideas, tied together through one common goal of highlighting the work of democracy through youth engagement. When gathering pieces for this anthology, we made an effort to reflect the amount of diversity we see in society today. In the pages that follow, then, you will see works from students of many backgrounds, gender identities, cultures, races, hometowns, etc. This anthology does not present you with one way of viewing current issues, one definition of where our generation stands on a current topic. Instead, this anthology offers a selection of rich ideas, plans of action, and experiences that we invite you to analyze, respond to, and accept or reject. Our goal is to foster dialogue and engagement among many voices, embedded within a "through line" of democratic possibilities.

The Lived Experience of Democracy: Criticizing Injustice, Building Community begins with a series of personal essays which make real the difficulty of navigating our culture through the experience of possessing an enriching culture, but having its value recognized in elementary, high school, or university classrooms. More than simply documenting the difficulty, however, we hope to have also demonstrated the strength and power of these writers to not only succeed but, through their personal example, expand the possibilities of those who follow. The essays then broaden in focus to explore how institutions can either continue these patterns of exclusion or transform into welcoming environments for the individuals and heritages that enrich their work. Here issues of democracy and justice intersect with issues such as healthcare, immigration, popular culture, and gun control. The final essays explore the shift from social awareness to cultural and political activism. This transition is signified by authors who've made specific calls to action on an individual and institutional level. The final essay is a meditation on the type of community possible if the visions expressed by these writers were to be realized.

If the final essay appears utopian, offering too perfect a vision of community, we make no apologies. For while the cultural and political issues discussed in this anthology appear unsolvable, these are also the issues our generation must solve. And we believe that the writers in this anthology demonstrate our generation's commitment to move entrenched issues into forward looking solutions, to break away from limiting stereotypes and exclusionary institutions, and to imagine a better future. Every generation is considered naïve, utopian in its beliefs, until, suddenly, it has changed the world.

"Every great dream begins with a dreamer. Always remember, you have within you the strength, the patience, and the passion to reach for the stars to change the world." - Harriet Tubman

CHAPTER ONE

What Lies Within a Name

Esha Fateh

"This young lady earned an A on the exam."

"Hey, you, why don't you explain this to the class?"

"Stellar work *points to me* on the project!"

For the entirety of a school year, my teacher did not utter my name. I was reduced to a series of improper nouns. My work was appreciated under a blanket of anonymity. One instance that has remained with me occurred when I raised my hand to answer a question. My teacher eyed me but was unsure about how to call on me. I peered back at my teacher, knowing what the problem was and nodded sympathetically. I was trying to communicate that it's alright to ask me my name, but I'm not sure if the message went through. After a moment of hesitation, my teacher resorted to pointing at me as a cue to answer.

One of the most fundamental aspects of human identity lies in a small phrase of letters that forms a name. Names provide the first glimpse of another culture when two different people meet for the first time. Correctly pronouncing an unfamiliar name is a critical first step that can help bridge an understanding. With growing divisions between cultural groups in society, it's now more important than ever to work towards building mutual respect. When I was born, my Pakistani grandparents gave a simple token of advice to my parents in search of a name to gift me: Make it short. A long name would be too difficult to pronounce, and I would spend my entire life correcting others. I ended up with a short four-letter name, but the goal in mind faltered within the first syllable. It's become a first day of school tradition. My teachers would try earnestly to call out unfamiliar names for attendance and a brief pause near the beginning of the list served as my cue to respond. Some of my teachers understood immediately and improved their pronunciation. Other teachers would hesitate to call me at all because they were unsure of the right pronunciation.

It is certainly not the case that educators purposely mispronounce the names of students unfamiliar to them. I've had teachers write small tips to help them sound names out. I've also had teachers in the past who were compelled to crop an unfamiliar name to just an initial. I've seen the flicker of discouragement that shines in my teachers' eyes when they erase the trailing letters of their names—symbols of their culture—to prevent confusion. The first step to address these issues lies in the proper pronunciation of unfamiliar names.

Society is the product of different groups coming together, each with their own perspectives to construct a diverse community of ideas. The different groups are like pillars as they hold society in place. It's important to study the groups to learn their views on topics that concern society as a whole. This is done by analyzing what major groups have done in regard to this issue in order to understand how receptive they would be to change. For the case of name pronunciation, the educational sector plays a role in introducing the concept of respecting other cultures to children. Some schools lack diversity and therefore have students face culture shock when they meet someone from a culture that is foreign to theirs. This cultural divide can carry well into adulthood and feed a polarizing society bent on misunderstanding.

Such long-term ramifications of this issue can be prevented in the classroom. Rather than pushing educators as the source of the problem, students can persuade educational leaders of the education pillar to listen by initiating conversations. For example, my teacher was likely hesitant on asking me how to pronounce my name because he was unsure how to ask. I understand his reservations since I was unsure how to ask others as well. By providing teachers with strategies on how to ask students the proper pronunciation of their names, teachers will be more comfortable with correcting their pronunciation because an obstacle will be removed for them. Likewise, for teachers with "unfamiliar last names," they should embrace their own full last name and not an initial. In this way, teachers can inspire students to embrace their identities and demonstrate to them how to respectfully ask for the right pronunciation. Conversations regarding the cultural origin of names and identity can start in the classroom to encourage an atmosphere of acceptance and respect.

To make this vision a reality, the initial step is in mobilizing support for correct name pronunciation in schools is by gaining the support of educators and administrators. This can be done by sharing experiences of students and educators that felt unseen due to mispronunciation. The next step might be choosing to purchase books that have characters with diverse names and backgrounds. This method would demonstrate to publishing companies that diverse characters and books from authors of color are in demand. Such books can help normalize correcting pronunciation of names in the classroom. In doing so, students learn the cultural importance behind names and grow to respect other cultures while proudly sharing aspects of their own culture. The third step would be to hire educators who can inspire their students to be respectful towards all cultures, which can ultimately help build connections between different racial groups and ethnicities. The students will grow into adults that are open-minded to learning how to pronounce and spell names that they are unfamiliar with and prevent misunderstandings that deepen divisions in society.

At the end of the day, this issue has a simple first step. The next time you meet with someone who has an unfamiliar name, look into their eyes and kindly ask for them to repeat it slowly. I greatly appreciate when someone takes a minute to learn the proper pronunciation of my name. It may seem daunting to ask, but the receiver will appreciate it. In doing so, you can spark a conversation that leaves a lasting connection based on mutual respect.

Esha Fateh is an undergraduate student at the University of Virginia interested in researching the intersections of the human brain, technology, and societal equity. She enjoys learning about a variety of topics through writing for the Cavalier Daily newspaper as a staff writer.

CHAPTER TWO

What Could've Been: Flaws in My Education

Niharika Singhvi

The first time I ever felt embarrassed about my culture happened on the first day of preschool. Up till then, I couldn't make the distinction between "tomorrow" and "yesterday." In Hindi, "kal" is used to refer to both with context revealing the intended meaning. Since my family had just moved from India a few weeks prior, I hadn't been able to fully grasp the concept of tomorrow when talking to my new U.S. classmates. So when my teacher told me to form a sentence about "the next day," I instead started rambling about the topic in the only way I knew how: in Hindi. In the following moments, as my peers shot me strange looks, I felt out of place–I was embarrassed and ashamed.

Although I only rarely faced that kind of upfront and dramatic action that made me feel belittled, I still experienced the subtle shaming that consistently reinforced this feeling of inferiority. For many years, I felt caught between a mental struggle of what I could bring to the table and what my peers would be willing to accept. Could I wear henna on my hands without the mockery I'd heard other students experienced? On a deeper level, could I share cultural thoughts and ideas I'd been raised with? In India, we're taught that if we accidentally step on a book, we should raise it to our heads as a sign of respect. This piece of Indian culture has shaped my respect for knowledge, and it could've been a valuable insight to bring to the table. So while I might have been welcomed and treated fairly as an individual, it was only because I learned to "fit in." Ultimately, that wasn't enough. I wanted to escape this burden of being afraid to express my culture, speak my language, share my heritage. I didn't want to fear how my classmates would react if I wore a traditional kurti on "country day" or if I brought dal and rice to school for lunch.

At least in my experience, educational institutions often fail to truly acknowledge the diversity that exists among their students. In her essay "From Candy Girls to Cyber Sistah-Cipher," Carmen Kynard explores this issue from the lens of a Black American woman. She explains how "it was not simply that school did not match the cultural and social capital of our families, communities, and peer stylings; it was that school actively disempowered what we brought to the table" (32). She argues that along with inbuilt racism, the nature of educational institutions in America limits students' expression of identity, particularly of those who are of a non-white race and a lower socio-economic class. It was this educational framework that caused my own cultural anxiety. The way we learned about our different student's cultures was chosen for us. It was a curriculum. It was systematic. Our knowledge about the backgrounds of our Black, Asian, and Native American peers was assessed by a multiple-choice exam where our teachers selected the content. I still remember learning about Hinduism in 8th grade. We were taught about sati and the caste system—some of the worst aspects of the religion but also practices that were outdated. I wish that we also had learned about the ideas of circular time and karma. Even if it lasted for half a lesson, these Hindu concepts could've challenged us to think about the world a little differently. But unfortunately, this content was already predetermined by a group of primarily white individuals in charge of the state's learning standards. And in the end, no matter what we learned, the material would still be a unit in the curriculum; once we turned in our exams, it was never integrated into the classroom, discussed, or emphasized in the student community.

Yet our upbringing, moral values, and political beliefs influence how we view the world. For example, in my high school *Theory of Knowledge* class, we'd often highlight how perspectives can change the content and reception of knowledge. My friends don't believe in reincarnation, but in my Jain community, it's widely accepted as a part of life. So if the two groups were to write about the topic, the opinions and facts they use—or at least the interpretation of them—are bound to differ. In a collectivist society like India, for example, there is a large emphasis on interpersonal relationships and family whereas in an individualistic society like America, independence and individuality are more valued. So when evaluating American history or even policies, our differing values are bound to result in varying perceptions and opinions. This discrepancy is why universities must emphasize the importance of identity. We are a product of our culture, nationality, education, and class. This background will necessarily play a role in how we think and act. And perhaps most importantly, for students to produce their best work, students must be able to acknowledge these factors to reduce their own bias, to truly display their persona, and to relay their thought process behind a work. Gloria Anzaldua, a prominent poet and feminist scholar, once wrote "I cannot separate my writing from any part of my life. It is all one" (394). For her, writing was like a trance, where words and ideas poured out of her, making the expression of her individuality a natural process. Similarly, students should be able to bring their individuality and background into their voice to maximize authenticity and originality in their work.

Students should not be held responsible for bringing this change, however. An individual student should not have to incorporate her identity into her work to make a school change. In the same essay, Kynard points out how Black women were often criticized for their unique dialect and would be punished by integrating it into their academic work. In other words, their individuality was questioned and rebuked solely because they were the minority in a university controlled by "whiteness," a term Kynard uses to describe the systemic racism of higher education. This led Kynard to question, "*What if* school success is really...about eradicating pan-African/black conscious identity and language or, at least, having to hide it and develop is somewhere else (which is still eradication)?" (41).

In fact, it's common for any minority—whether it's individuals of a lower class, different race, or different sexuality—to feel pressured to conform. I felt this pressure growing up when I chose to change myself to fit in with my white peers. As a student, it's also in my nature to conform. As do many others, I want to get good grades and eventually a stable job which is why I attempt to replicate the writing we read and the content we're taught in my work. Why would I force my identity as a middle-class Indian American student into my history paper when I can safely mimic academic writing and score an A? Do I really need to learn about jugaad and other untranslatable ideas if I can get into college without them? My own mentality represents a failure of my education. I've always considered a successful student to be someone who follows convention and serves to impress our teachers. But ideally, students would be encouraged to not only learn traditionally but also to integrate their individuality to work towards what they believe. Which is to say, change must not be expected from the actions of individual students in individual classes; change must occur at the root of the problem—educational institutions.

At the minimum, universities must allow students to be the type of intellectual which expresses their values. No student should feel compelled to talk about their cultural roots, but they should have the choice to do so. Currently, rigid educational structures restrict this possibility. Stringent rubrics and outlined expectations encourage homogeneity among students and prevent them from going out of the box to express their creativity. Up till now, unless an assignment specifically stated otherwise, I never felt like I had the space for personal cultural expression. If I was told to write about character development, I would stick to the script and talk about what we'd learned in class. My teachers' rubrics and grading reflected that that was the path to the best answer. However, maybe if I was encouraged to bring in a more cultural perspective, I could talk about characters' development in terms of their respect for elders or bonds with their families. This would result in a more holistic and distinct analysis. If assignments and corresponding rubrics were made to be more inclusive, I'd feel more comfortable sharing myself through my work while also contributing uniquely to the thoughts and ideas that shape our learning.

But beyond adjustments in the classroom, there needs to be broader institutional change. Minority students in America often encounter predominantly white administration and faculty. Even in my K-12 education, I never had a teacher of color—excluding substitute teachers. Moreover, we also attend universities run by those unlike us, inherently affecting the way our identity is treated. Even now, diversity is praised; colleges take pride in their demographics. But if diversity is treated like something special, it can't be wholly integrated. Instead, the expression of my identity and that of my peers must become the norm. The change we want and the values we stand for must be taught and incorporated into the classrooms where we learn. Along with talking about biblical references in English literature, I want my teachers to explore books from around the world and talk about the dozens of other religions represented among their students, like Hinduism. In the end, I don't need people to adapt to my cultural values and background. I don't even need them to understand them fully. I just want to feel comfortable expressing my personal experiences, my culture, and my identity. For this to occur, universities must find a balance within the diversity that exists on their campus. Instead of one group, individual, or minority having to conform to another side or vice versa, everyone should find a middle ground where our identities are acknowledged and appreciated.

Ultimately, I'm not here to offer a solution to these vital problems but rather to emphasize that one must be found. More nuanced and open-minded rubrics, assignments surrounding identity, and discussion of diversity are only a start. But for students to legitimately feel comfortable with writing their own stories on paper, diversity can no longer be downplayed as a data figure or an asset. Its value and expression must be accepted as an ordinary aspect of our classrooms and coursework. When that happens, preschoolers like my 5-year-old self wouldn't feel isolated because of where they came from; they'd feel welcomed.

But evolving our education system isn't just beneficial for 5-year-old Niharika. It's also important for the 19-year-old version of myself who still sometimes feels embarrassed speaking Hindi in public. It's important for the numerous other individuals who've felt uncomfortable or even ashamed of sharing their culture, their identity. On a larger scale, institutional changes can help thousands of students be more open-minded and empathetic to the backgrounds and struggles of others. Since our education is so fundamental to our growth, these changes can help ingrain unity and acceptance from an early age, which is critical for political advancement. Cultural diversity is such a beautiful and enriching truth of America. I only wish for others to see and accept that.

WORKS CITED

Kynard, Carmen. "From Candy Girls to Cyber Sistah Cypher: Narrating Black Females' Color Consciousness and Counterstories in *and* out of School." *Harvard Educational Review*. Vol. 80. No. 1. Spring 2010. 30-52.

CHAPTER THREE
Ni Hao

Chris Allen

The classroom makes me feel as if I have been transported to my elementary school days. The white linoleum floor, the alphabet above the whiteboard, the globe in the corner, and drawings showing different types of weather all take me back. However, instead of children, the class is full of adults, refugees from a multitude of places who have come together to learn English. Today we are talking about our families. As it is my first day as a teaching assistant, I get to go first. I launch into a monologue about my history, parents, and younger sister, but I quickly realize that I have lost everyone. I backtrack and start over but again am soon met with blank stares. I then try one last time, now cutting out everything but the most basic information. Finally, people understand me.

We then go around the room, everyone saying a few halting words about their families, from the two Liberians, an El Salvadoran, and a Tibetan on the left; to the handful of Syrians in the back; and contingent of Afghans, a Congolese man, and a Filipino woman on the right.

Despite the familiar classroom setting, the stories seem alien. While the **beginning** English makes it difficult for me to understand everything, I hear parts of stories about growing-up with fourteen siblings to living as a subsistence farmer. The most striking response, however, comes from Mohammed, a Syrian man and one of the more elderly in the class (I have not used people's real names in this essay). He has already appointed himself class clown, whispering Arabic jokes to his tablemates and acting pantomimes for the non-Arabic speakers. When it is his turn to speak, he becomes somber and mimes shooting a gun. Despite the teacher's insistence, he refuses to provide more details and class continues as "normal." As I grew closer to Mohammed over the next few weeks, he eventually tells me that he had three sons back home in Syria, all of whom were killed in the war. He also shows me pictures of them, which are always kept in his wallet. Nevertheless, Mohammed still keeps everyone laughing when he comes to class every week.

**

Each weekday, I spend an hour in a classroom that looks very different to the one where I volunteer. Instead of the colorful posters depicting weather, the walls are bare except for a rarely used blackboard and a projector. It is the classroom for my introductory Mandarin Chinese course. Over the next year, it will serve both as a haven from the outside world and the source of much distress.

My first day of Chinese class is only a few weeks before my first TA session with the refugees. The seats in the class are a desk-chair combination on wheels. All of my classmates and I have subconsciously rolled ourselves into the back corners, away from the projector. As we huddle there together, waiting for class to begin, we start talking. We chat about who we are, where we are from, and why we are studying Chinese. The first thing I realize is that almost everyone has a connection to China in some way. Some people lived in China, others studied Chinese in high school, and one person is dating someone from China.

Then the professor walks in, with a friendly *ni hao*. This is one expression we all know—*how are you*?—so he is met with an energetic chorus of ni hao's. He introduces himself as Teacher Li, says that he arrived recently in the United States for the first time, and that he is excited to learn about the University with us. He quickly charms the class with pictures of his newborn baby and his nervous enthusiasm. Bit by bit, my classmates and I roll our desks towards the front of the room, ready to start learning.

Our first lesson is about family. Like many things in Chinese, it starts off easily enough. 妈妈 or *ma-ma* are the characters for mother and

爸爸 or *ba-ba* are the characters for father. Over the next few days, we continue learning new characters and sentence structures. As soon as we have seemingly mastered talking about our families, more depth is added. To my horror, I learn that Chinese family-related vocabulary is so expansive that there is even a unique word for the wife of the brother of your paternal grandfather.

Eventually, Teacher Li feels that we are ready to be let loose to discuss the topics among ourselves. There is just one rule: *Chinese only.* I turn around to another first-year student to start applying what we have learned. When discussion starts, the innate sensibilities of our first-language is quickly lost. Our senses of humor instantly click. Whether it be "我爱你" (*I love you*) or "我觉得你爸爸很漂亮" (*I think your father is very pretty*), phrases that would never be uttered in English begin to fly around the classroom. When faced with a task as daunting as learning ten distinct words for different types of cousins, what else can you do to keep your sanity?

**

The second Tuesday of volunteering with refugees is spent practicing introductions. We start class with me and my fellow TA demonstrating proper introduction technique: a firm handshake and then, "Hello, my name is Chris Allen. What is your name?" and "It is nice to meet you, I am from Northern Virginia and am a student at the University of Virginia here in Charlottesville." After this, the class stands up and gets in two lines. Like reverse gunslingers, one pair at a time we take three paces towards each other and stick out their hands. With the pressure of everyone watching, some people's introductions are inaudible, quivering, or masked by nervous giggles. We go down the line until everyone has met his or her partner, then shift down so everyone has a new partner, and then repeat the exercise.
The monotony of class is broken when someone's phone rings. It is Ahmed's, a Syrian man in his early 30s. He excuses himself to take the phone call but comes back a short while later with a confused look. He gives me his phone and motions for me to listen. Unsure of the procedure in this situation, I hesitantly do so.

The first thing I realize is that I am listening to an automated message and, second, that the message is coming from a hospital. In English, the voice briskly outlines the time, location, and items to bring for a scheduled appointment. I replay the message several times, try to communicate with Ahmed, and eventually write down the necessary information. I piece together that the appointment is for his brother, who had been very ill recently.

While I try to help as much as I can, it will still be an incredibly difficult road for Ahmed and his brother. How will they find the appointment's location within the hospital, communicate their problems, and discuss payment or insurance in a place and language completely foreign to them? What if I or another English speaker was not nearby when that call came in? For members of the class, every single day is filled with struggles such as this. Even something as simple as going shopping can be cripplingly intimidating.

**

Over the first weeks of school, my Chinese class quickly learned not to mistake our teacher's eagerness and kindness for weakness. Class accelerated at a relentless pace, with at least two hours of daily homework on top of class time. Each student began to realize that the complexity of learning a new language, especially one like Chinese, is unlike other academic challenges. The persistence and time required mean your chosen new language is always with you. For me, this has manifested in muttering Chinese phrases to myself, dreaming of homework assignments, and attempting to eavesdrop on any Chinese conversation within earshot. Throughout this process, each person in my class found their motivation for studying Chinese strained, often to the breaking point. From that first class to the end of second semester, our class size dropped from twenty people to eleven.

I am lucky in that my motivation, stemming partly from my childhood, held strong. From when I was 6-years-old until I was 9-years-old, my family lived in Beijing due to my father's assignment there with the U.S. Foreign Service. I remember riding the school bus every day from my family's home inside Beijing's Third Ring Road to my school that was outside the Fourth Ring Road. For the entire journey, which could last as short as 30 minutes or as long as one and a half hours depending on traffic, I would stare out the window. It was fascinating to watch the transition from the urban city center, choking with new construction, to the more rustic feel near my school, where mopeds buzzed by, en route to market with a dozen squawking chickens strapped on.

My other main source of motivation is my father, whose Chinese proficiency has been very beneficial for him throughout his career. But equally as impactful for me are the interactions he has with people. In many situations, from ordering food in Chinese restaurants to chatting with Chinese tourists, he simply says a few lines and can quickly make connections with people who understand the effort required to successfully wrangle with the language. Considering that he only started to study Chinese after college, it is inspiring. Surely I, too, can master it – if I just keep working hard.

**

On occasion, the mix of cultures stuffed in a room together would produce results straight from a comedy sketch. One day, we are again discussing where we come from. A soft-spoken young man from Vietnam is presenting in front of the class.

"I am Dai. I'm from Vietnam."

Quietly at first, but quickly growing in volume, chatter erupts from the back corner of the room where a group of older African women has congregated. Dai looks up and stops talking.

"No, you are from Mexico," a voice emerges from the group.

"I'm from Vietnam!" he protests.

"No, but he speaks Spanish," one of the women articulates the group's sentiments. This is not true; Dai speaks Vietnamese and has never spoken a word of Spanish in his life.

Dai seems taken aback by this suggestion, but he is outnumbered and appears to be resigning himself to being Mexican. While I normally take a back seat in class discussions, I feel that it is time to come to his defense. I do my best to convince the class that Dai is, in fact, from

Vietnam. For the rest of the semester, every time he speaks, the class fills with mutterings about Spanish and Mexicans.

**

Another reason I have been able to stay dedicated to my Chinese class is because it is so structured. Every day, we learn five to ten new characters that we know will be tested in the next class. Unlike other classes, where one can theoretically go weeks without showing up or doing the reading before feeling the impact, if one misses even a single day of Chinese, you will have to work three times as hard to catch up again—especially when we began building off of old characters and grammar structures, maintaining the pace of the class became crucial. If you did keep up, you quickly realized that Chinese grammar itself is not very different from that of English. It is relatively straightforward, with a lack of verb tenses and genders. The most interesting thing for me has been seeing how characters combine in different contexts to make new words. For example, 电 means "electricity" on its own and 脑 is defined as "head," but the two together mean "computer." Once one starts to see the basic underlying logical patterns that tie the language together, it is easier and far more enjoyable to learn.

These processes were on full display in a paper that a Chinese hall-mate asked me to edit. The paper, an advanced philosophy paper, was my hall-mate's attempt to disprove the theory of time. While his argument raced past my understanding in the first few paragraphs, the grammatical mistakes were interesting as they were the exact opposite of the mistakes that I was making in Chinese class. For example, the lack of articles in Chinese was a tough concept to familiarize myself with; missing articles made up roughly 40% of the mistakes in my hall-mate's paper. Another 40% of his mistakes were subject-verb disagreements, a concept one does not need to worry about in Chinese. After an hour of scrutinizing his paper, I felt exhausted by the fickleness of English and appreciated the relatively clean sensibilities of Chinese grammar.

**

At the start of my second semester volunteering, I was moved to a more advanced class. It was quite a change, coming from a class where some people had been in the United States for only a few weeks and in which we once spent thirty minutes discussing the meaning of the word "title" (I tried to do this by explaining that I had a name, Chris, and that the title of the short story we were reading was essentially its name).

Walking into class the first day seemed very familiar, with colorful posters on the walls and students. As the teacher begins class, I sit down at a table with a South Korean, an Afghan, and an El Salvadoran. She announces that class will begin with a one-page reading on politics, something that would not be feasible in my original class. The trio at my table take turns reading sentences aloud, with me providing help with pronunciations or definitions when needed.

After fifteen minutes of reading and a quick discussion, we jump into our main topic of the day—reasons for studying English. Immediately, the room fills with chatter; everyone can talk about learning English. The optimism is tangible. At my table, I hear plans to go to college, bring family to the United States, get a well-paying job, and move to a big city. All want to settle down in the United States. Every single person emphasizes, more than anything else, the ideal of creating a better life for his or her children. The proud Afghan tells about her daughter who is studying introductory Chinese at a local middle school and gets "90 to 100" on all of her tests. Like every parent, these people see their children as their future and a way to make a mark on the world.

There is one voice of disillusionment though. It comes from a West African man sitting at the table neighboring mine. I had already noticed him due to the way he was dressed. Everyone else is either in traditional dress or casual clothes, but he wears a freshly dry-cleaned suit and exudes the confidence of a professor. He is telling his tablemates he has realized it is impossible to improve one's standing in society and is advocating for everyone to downsize their goals. People are not sure what to make of this and start to become frightened. My fellow TA sits down at his table and starts talking with him. He tells her that his name is Victor, and he was a practicing doctor with a medical degree in his home country of Nigeria. When he arrived in Charlottesville four years ago, he quickly realized that the American medical community did not appreciate his degree from a Nigerian university and his lack of conversational English. He tells my co-volunteer that he is trying to regain some of the social standing and dignity of his past life but is facing many cultural and language roadblocks. He quietly mutters about trying to find a job, but with no family on the East Coast and the current political climate, he is struggling to maintain hope for the future. She empathizes with him but argues that these are not reasons to stop fighting and improve himself.

In the car ride home, my friend is visibly shaken. Given the circumstances, she had done a great job of talking with Victor about his frustrations and giving him perspective, but she is upset from the ordeal. As a young Muslim woman herself, she is all too aware of the unfairness in our society and feels the truth in what Victor was saying.

**

The next week, during our fifteen-minute break in the middle of class, I meander between groups of people, trying to get to know my new students. I start talking to an older lady named Lilly who, to my great excitement, is Chinese.

"I am actually studying Mandarin right now."

"Ahhh, that is interesting," her skepticism is easily visible.

"I have taken it for the past year, I am really enjoying it, but it is very hard," I mumble in the best Chinese I can manage.

Her face is a mixture of surprise and confusion, as she tries to understand my Chinese, but is not entirely sure what I am saying. "I think you speak very good. How do you say hello in Chinese?" Lilly asked, still in English.

"Ni hao."

"You are so good at Chinese," she says enthusiastically, still preferring to speak in English.

"Thank you, I think you speak very good English," I respond slowly in Chinese.

"No, I can understand things, but my speaking is very bad."

I pause, desperately trying to think of something to say. I then remember our current lesson in Chinese. "What sport do you like to play?"

"我很喜欢乒乓" she says, much faster than I can comprehend. She repeats in English, "I like to play ping pong. In high school, I was the best player in my school and traveled all around China in tournaments."

We go back and forth in this manner for a little while, with me trying to speak Chinese and her responding in English. The conversation does not move fast as we both are pushed to the limits of our new languages. "My grammar is bad, but you understand me. Sometimes your grammar is bad, but I understand you," she says proudly.

When one of us gets stuck, the other person repeats the question more slowly. If that does not work, the other explains the answer. When we are finally on the same page again, we start giggling like children on a playground and repeat the new phrase back and forth. Over the remainder of the break, we talk, and then meet up again after class to continue our conversation. I bring up as many topics as I can remember from my Chinese class, but eventually we are torn apart as my fellow volunteers are anxious to leave after our three-hour shift.

I am giddy for the whole car ride back to my dorm. For one, actually being able to use Chinese in the "real world" (albeit in a very limited way) is encouraging. Especially at a time when I have grown used to only using it in the confines of the classroom where it is easy to lose track of progress.

I also begin to think of my students' journeys with English in the same context as my struggles with Chinese. While I am cursing the complexities of tones in Chinese, they are probably doing the same with English grammar.

But in many ways, it is not fair to compare our attempts to master a new language. First, my students must have a much more difficult time than I do. As adults, they naturally struggle to learn languages more than someone whose brain is still developing. I like to think that I'm a fairly involved college student, but many of these people are looking after several families' children or working multiple jobs in addition to learning English. Also, Chinese is becoming my second language while many of my students already know three or four.

But most importantly, the people to whom I teach English do not have the same intrinsic interest in learning their new language that I do. More than likely, they would have been very happy to live a quiet life in their own country without any interaction with the West or English speakers. Instead, a series of unintended and often horrific events and circumstances have put them in a situation where they are virtually forced to learn this new language. Furthermore, the more they become invested in American culture and English, the more that they are casting aside their own cultures.

Regardless of one's political views about new immigrants coming into the country, it is in everyone's best interest to support those who are already here. The impression I have from the refugees whom I have taught is the malleability of their perception of America. They arrive with high hopes but do not really know what to expect. If their reception is warm and welcoming, they will respond likewise. But if they are shunned by society and not given opportunities to thrive—never mind the basic tools to survive—they could quickly become disillusioned, like Victor. This is why I believe that easing refugees such as my classmates into American culture through programs such as the ones in which I volunteer is so important. Even with this assimilation, I worry for the students. If everything goes as well as possible for them, they may acquire an intermediate level of conversational English, get a GED, find a basic white-collar job, and hope that they have been able to give their children the tools to make it to college. Nevertheless, the cheerful and lively discussions with Mohammed, Ahmed, Dai, Victor, Lilly, and all the others is a weekly highlight for me. By incorporating fun into our hard work, we slowly but doggedly climb up the seemingly insurmountable challenge of acquiring a new language.

Chris Allen graduated from UVA in 2020 with a major in Commerce. Since graduating, he has moved to Johannesburg, South Africa, to work in investing although he still misses the UVA and Charlottesville communities. Throughout his time at the university, he volunteered with the Madison House English for Speakers of Other Languages program, which became a defining part of his experience.

CHAPTER FOUR

Fourteen Year Difference

Mariam Mohamed

It's my first day of being an ESL (English as a Second Language) tutor. I am as excited but also as nervous as a freshman student starting their first day of high school. I am wearing a yellow shirt with jeans and black boots. I'm looking well put-together but deep down feeling anxious. I am not sure what to expect or how I will be as a tutor. I am nervous that I won't be able to explain things in a way the ESL students will understand. I arrive at Upper Walker Elementary School and go to Ms. H's ESL classroom. I introduce myself by saying, "Hi everyone, my name is Mariam Mohamed. I am a second-year student at The University of Virginia. I currently live in Northern Virginia but was born in Egypt." I look around the classroom and see two Hijabi girls getting excited to see that I wear the hijab, too. I smile and take a seat next to one of the Hijabi students named Aaina. She is using a school-issued laptop and borrows pencils and papers from the teacher. I can tell by the way she is dressed and by the way she is having to borrow basic school supplies from the teacher that her family is struggling financially. My smile slowly starts fading away as my eyes try to hold tears back as I start to remember how the struggle felt.

Fourteen years ago, I was Aaina. Fourteen years ago, my parents took my brothers and I on a journey to a place we never even knew existed. From Cairo, Egypt to Brooklyn, New York. I remember being confused as to why we were here, where my cousins, aunts, and grandparents were. I was confused why no one around me was wearing the hijab like my mom or why no one around me spoke the only language I knew—Arabic. I remember the apartment we lived in was so small that I hated it because we had so much better in Egypt. I remember going shopping with my mom and only buying clothes that were on sale because we did not have enough money to buy clothes that actually looked good. We barely had money. We did not have money to buy basic school supplies because I remember having to always borrow pencils from the teacher. Money was so limited that my mom would only buy things that were considered "necessary." That included things like groceries and clothes but excluded things like toys. For the longest, America felt like the worst place to live. All I could think about was how I wished to be back in Egypt

I remember during every lunch period, there was always the girls table and the boys table. While the boys were fighting with mini-wrestling figures on finger skateboards, the girls were all peacefully playing with these little pet figures called the Littlest Pet Shops. I couldn't play with the girls. Not only didn't I know how to speak English, I also did not have a Littlest Pet Shop, so I felt very excluded. One day after school, my mom and I went shopping for clothes. I was getting bored of her just staring at clothes, so I wandered off to the toy section. Not surprisingly, I found Littlest Pet Shops being sold for $15 per animal figure. I picked up the cute brown dog that had a pink bowtie and made my way to my mom. I was nervous to ask her if I could buy it, but I decided to take the risk anyway. I wanted to be like the girls in school. So I asked her, but after I told her the price, she told me to "Put it back that is unnecessary." Unnecessary? That piece of plastic that every girl has is *unnecessary*? Me trying to buy something so I can fit in and have friends is *unnecessary*? I was broken, saddened, and destroyed. I felt like I was never going to be able to make friends with the way life was going. Here I was, this girl who didn't speak or understand English, who could barely afford anything, and who had no friends to talk to at school.

I see my childhood self in the eyes of these students.

After settling down in Ms. H's classroom, she pairs up students with a tutor. Since I am already sitting next to Aaina, Ms. H assigns me to work with her. She opens up her school-issued laptop and goes on the online reading website they use in class. She picks any random book and starts listening to the audio of the book to get a good understanding of how the words are pronounced. After the audio is done, I decide to read it out loud to her so she can hear how the words are pronounced again. I ask her to read after I am done, and she does just that. However, I start hearing sniffles between every other word. I am confused because just a few minutes ago she was fine. I ask her what's wrong, but she whispers under her breath, "Nothing." I am not really sure what to do other than just be physically there for her. I passed her a tissue and just sat there next to her for a few minutes. I then ask her if she wants to take a walk with me outside, and she agrees to do so.

We leave the classroom and start making our way towards the playground. As we are walking, all I can think about is whether or not to ask her again what's wrong. I do not want to seem like the pushy tutor/teacher who forces you to speak on something you don't feel comfortable sharing. I decided that it would be better to just get her in a better mood rather than making her talk about something that upsets her.

I look at her and say, "Aaina! Tell me, where are you from?"

She responds with, "I'm from Afghanistan."

I then say, "No way! I've never been to Afghanistan, but I heard the mountains there are beautiful." She continues to talk about Afghanistan and the culture in Afghanistan which I then related to her by saying
"Ya, you know I am from Egypt, and over there the kids always play soccer in the middle of the streets, too."

We go back and forth about Afghanistan and Egypt, their similarities and differences, and how we miss our home countries. Luckily for me, this conversation dries Aaina's tears as she is able to talk about something that brings her happiness. Not only did I want to show Aaina that we are similar in the sense that we are both immigrants, I wanted to show her that I am not much older than her and that she should view me as a friend rather than a tutor/teacher. I could not think of any other way to do so than by sharing that I have a little brother around her age and all the stuff that he does. We start talking about *Roblox* (an online game that is popular among middle schoolers), YouTube channels, and "stupid" comebacks that 6th graders say. She starts laughing when I would tell her about how my little brother annoys me and all the fights that we have. She then shares stories about her and her siblings and how some of the older ones are still in Afghanistan.

"My older brother is at school in Afghanistan. He did not come with us here because he has to finish school and take care of my grandma," she says.

"Do you miss him?" I respond.

"Ya, but I call him on FaceTime, and he shows me my grandma, too," she continues.

After we walked about three laps around the playground, Aaina really seems to be in a good mood to go back to class and continue reading. We go back to the classroom, and she is able to continue reading with ease.

The walk that I had with Aaina probably meant more to me than it did to her. While walking, all I could think about was my older brother Ahmed and when we first moved to New York. Although Ahmed and I started in the same elementary school when we first got to America, we both had different experiences. I came when I was a kindergarten, but he was a second grader. Fortunately for me, my kindergarten class was not really mean or nice; they just left me alone. However, Ahmed's second grade class was basically the class of bullies. For example, during the first month of school, Ahmed still did not have a backpack. One day, my mom and he went shopping for one. They went to Payless and saw a backpack with who we know now as *Dora the Explorer*. Due to the culture difference here in America and in Egypt, both my mom and brother thought that Dora was a guy character because girls in Egypt rarely have really really short hair. Over there, short hair is known to be a boy style, so many girls did not want to cut their hair short because they did not want to look like a boy. To my brother and mom, the backpack was just some random little boy who is adorable. They purchased that backpack for my brother, and he went to school with it the next day. Every day that week my mom would get a call from the principal that Ahmed was crying and that they could not get him to say why. Time passed until my mom finally figured out that many of his classmates were making fun of not only his backpack but not being able to speak English. Ahmed said his classmates would always say things to him that he did not understand, and then laugh together about it. This almost seemed like a scene from a movie, but unfortunately it was just the reality that Ahmed had to face. The bullying continued throughout the months, for different reasons every day. Ahmed dealt with getting made fun of, being called names he didn't understand, and getting his lunch stolen from time to time by a fifth grader.

During my walk with Aaina, I could not help but think that maybe she is sad because of the way someone in that school was treating her. Maybe it is because she is tired of being like an outsider because of the way she speaks English. Maybe it is because she misses the comfortable lifestyle she was used to in Afghanistan. Or maybe she has personal problems happening at home that affect her directly. The cause of Aaina's and Ahmed's tears may or may not have been for the same reason, but the thing they share is that they were both immigrant students who had to deal with the American education system/public school while barely knowing English. A lot of times, teachers underestimate how much immigrant students go through both at home and at school. They just expect them to "give it their all" on school assignments. In a perfect world, a student would put their best efforts in all assignments, but the reality is that immigrant students deal with a lot of personal problems, such as adapting to the new change, family problems, or bullies that can distract them from learning.

I still remember the day I had to go to school after the night our house got robbed. It was during the wintertime. My mom, Ahmed, and I were coming back from grocery shopping. I was getting better at adapting to our new "home" even though it was not considered home for me. I remember that night very clearly. I was wearing a really big stuffed pink jacket and a scarf my mom forced me to wear around my nose and mouth. I was holding my mom's hand as we were walking back home. I remember Ahmed and I were talking about how we really need to go to the bathroom because we could barely hold it in. We finally saw the house and I could not be happier that I was going to be able to use the bathroom. As we got closer to the house, my mom's face turned into fear and confusion. She stopped walking and stood in silence. I was confused and started throwing a fit because

I really needed to go to the bathroom. She told me that I needed to stop whining and that we could not enter the house because it was not safe. I was not sure what she meant but I just followed her lead as she turned the other direction and started making phone calls. What I did not know at that time was that someone had broken our main window, got into the house, and stole the TV along with other items that my mom never told me about.

For one week straight, we had a big black trash bag taped to cover the broken window. Every night that week I slept in fear that a random man was going to walk into the house and take more belongings, or even worse—kill us. The feeling of fear was beyond what I can describe and that killed me emotionally and mentally. Yet, every morning that week I had to get out of bed and go to school like everything was fine at home. I had to pretend like I did not live in fear and just go and focus on learning English. I tried to focus but a lot of my teachers did not realize that I was not able to concentrate on classwork because my mind was just busy thinking about if my parents were safe at home. I had no motivation to learn in school that week because I was just looking at the clock, waiting to see if my mom survived to pick me up that day. This "home" was not safe at all. I had to live with that fear for the reminder of the time spent living in Brooklyn.

Although I think it's safe to say that Charlottesville, Virginia is safer than Brooklyn, New York, as a tutor you cannot disregard the struggles of these ESL students as their struggles come in a different form other than living in danger. One of my ESL students named Layla has a lot of behavioral problems. Tutoring her comes with the challenge that you first have to get past her attitude and talk backs, and *then* get her to sit and focus on her work. Prior to this particular day, Layla was always talking back to her teachers, not raising her hand, bothering other students, and walking out of the classroom. Usually, Ms. H handles Layla's behavior with special care by staying as calm as possible and talking to her nicely, even if she is rude to her. However, that day, Layla was having a verbal altercation with the PE teacher. He starts yelling at Layla in front of her classmates and tutors. He points out that she needs to lose the attitude. Obviously, Layla does not take that well. She starts to talk back as she is not willing to step back from the argument. The two go back and forth, yelling at each other in front of everyone. Layla then feels embarrassed that she is getting yelled at and put on the spot, so she starts to cry and tells him that he does not know what she has gone through.

As her classmates make their way to PE, Layla refuses to go because she is still angered up with emotions. I sit next to her, and I ask her what's wrong. She starts talking about how the PE teacher is so mean to her and that, "He is not my parent to yell at me like that." I let her rant about him for a couple more seconds, and I then asked her what she meant by "You don't know what I go through." She opens up to me and shares that she is the oldest of 6 kids and that her mom has placed a lot of expectations on her. She continues to say that she has to help take care of her siblings, clean, and do homework. She says that it is very hard and stressful because she does not have as much time as any other student to study or focus on homework. She adds that most of the time she does not do her homework, which results in teachers getting mad at her. It almost feels like a repeating cycle of having a lot of responsibilities at home, not having time to do your homework, and then getting yelled at by the teacher.

Now that I know this about Layla, I am more careful about the ways I approach her during each tutoring session. For example, today I have to help Layla complete her math packet that is about multiplication. It is about six pages long, which Layla is already mad about, but I tell her that if she stays on task, then I will play basketball with her afterwards. She seems happy to do so, so we begin right away. She does the first two pages with me, and then I start to see that she is losing interest. She is getting distracted by talking to other students.

I tell her, "Come on, we want to make sure we have enough time to play basketball."

She responds with, "But I have a blister. I don't want to write."

I thought about what the best thing to do is and I came to the realization that I can be her writing hand as long as she tells me what to write, word for word. I realize that by doing so, she will be able to focus on the material itself rather than putting her attention on her handwriting or how much her hand hurts. We did just that and we were able to finish the assignment in a timely manner with no attitude or behavioral problems along the way.

Crossing boundaries by pushing a student too much can result in students being frustrated with the idea of learning something new, not wanting to try new things, or even hating the subject throughout their academic career. Speaking from personal experience, I have been affected by teachers crossing my boundaries when I was younger. More specifically, when I was in the ESL program, I was always forced to read, read, and read. There were a lot of days that I was upset at school because my parents back at home were financially stressed. I carried a lot on my plate as a kindergartener as I felt responsible for actions that my parents took. To this day, I feel like this financial stress and adapting to the new environment has made me mature quicker because I was forced to care about "grown-up" things rather than focusing my time on playing with toys like Littlest Pet Shop.

During my time as an ESL student, I personally felt like my ESL teacher did not care about me as a person, just as a student. Her only goal was to teach me how to write, speak, read, and understand English. I do not remember her once asking me about how life at home was or what Egypt was like. It was always just, "Read this. Write this. Read it again." I hated going to ESL class with a passion. This feeling is not something a student is born with but rather grows to adopt. For me, ESL became the class that I never got a break in and always had to read and write. I remember I would have days where I was feeling down, and my teacher always just gave me books to read. Her routine was that she read the book once to me, and then I read back to her. I was a very very slow reader, as one can assume so, and she made me feel bad about it. Sometimes she would tell me I was doing a "good job," but other times I would have to "pick up the pace." I felt like I was trying my hardest to improve, but she was just not pleased. It angered me at times because at some points it made me feel like I will never be able to read as a regular person would because I had to sit here and pronounce most of the words on the page. It seemed unfair because I worked twice as hard as the students in my grade, but they were reading books with ease while I felt like reading a few pages took me years.

As I got older and was now in second grade, my English vocabulary became richer. I was still in ESL, but a lot of my classes were with the native-English speakers. I was getting better at reading faster, but I was still slower than an average student. Yet as I got older, my hate towards reading grew as there was now another problem. Not only did my teacher always tell me to pick up the pace, but she now wanted me to practice reading out loud to the class. As if she already did not cross the boundary before, she now made me do something way out of my comfort zone. I have always felt embarrassed to read out loud to the class because I feel like I am reading slowly and pronouncing some words wrong. To this day, I still hate reading out loud because of the fear that I had when I was younger—that someone was going to make fun of the way I read. This is what I mean when I say that teachers/tutors should be careful when pushing students to excel because too much can lead them to develop long-lasting hate.

Since I personally experienced being pushed out of my comfort zone when I was an ESL student, I am always very cautious with how I go about tutoring my students. For example, I tutor a girl from El Salvador named Genesis. We are doing a reading exercise that involves having to read over and over again. Because I hated when my ESL teacher never gave me breaks, I made sure that I would give Genesis breaks after reading a book twice. During our break, I either let her relax for two minutes or talk to me about anything she wants. I need to make sure that she is able to clear her mind again before resuming to the next task or else she will develop a hateful relationship with reading. I also make sure to guide her through big words that are difficult to pronounce and reassure her that she is doing a good job trying with the big words. As an ESL tutor, I personally want Genesis to improve her speaking, writing, reading, and understanding of the English language, but I know that it is best if I don't put a time limit on this goal. In other words, every student learns at a different pace, and that is completely fine. Trying to rush a student to learn will never help reach the end goal, so take time to let the students relax and refresh so that they are ready to learn more and more.

Another thing that I am always cautious about when tutoring these ESL students is not telling them how to spell a word right away. I want my students to try and sound out the letters and write what they think the letters are before asking me how to spell a certain word. I did this because when I was an ESL student, my teacher always helped me with spelling. I would barely have to try, and she would tell me the correct way of spelling a word. Although I appreciated it then, that method of teaching did not help me in the long run because it never really taught me how to spell. To this day, I struggle to spell words and can only be grateful that we have autocorrect because if I had to hand write everything, all the words would be misspelled.

One big difference from what I experienced as an ESL student versus what my ESL students experience is inclusion. When looking at ESL students, one is always trying to answer the question: what approaches/methods of teaching are the most effective? There will be studies that show that having one-on-one tutoring is best, other studies that say place them in regular classrooms as they will learn from their peers; however, I disagree with both. Being an ESL student myself and an ESL tutor, I believe that the best way to go about this is having a class period set for ESL students to be together in a classroom. In this case, students will still be able to be with native speakers in all their other classes but have more time to practice English during their ESL class period. This way the ESL students will not feel alone and separated as they will be in a classroom full of other ESL students. This method was used at Upper Walker Elementary School as they have all the fifth and sixth grade ESL students placed in the same ESL class period for one-and-a-half hours a day. By being amongst other ESL students, each student felt a sense of community as they realized that they are not alone in this journey of learning and understanding English. The students at Upper Walker Elementary School still experienced being in English-speaking classrooms, ESL classrooms, *and* had enough time for recess. These students got the break that I never experienced before.

I believe that this is the most effective way because growing up as an ESL student, I was taken out of recess time to sit one on one with a teacher in a very small classroom. As a kindergartner, recess time meant everything, and the fact that I was pulled away from that to do more schoolwork while my classmates had fun playing with the sandbox already made me hate learning English. It seemed unfair to me that I had to do double the work and still not have time to play. I remember the feeling of sadness that I felt every time I saw my ESL teacher come to pick me up as soon as it was recess time. I wished I was in the classroom fighting over which baby doll I wanted to play with or who was going to be the mom and dad when it came to playing family. I wished I was in the classroom to see the boys run around and play tag or pretend to shoot each other as another form of a live action game. Instead, I had to stare at pieces of paper with pictures of objects that I now know as cars, trees, flowers, and houses. It almost felt like I was being punished for not being able to speak English. I know that was not the intention, but as a five-year-old, taking away recess was a form of being punished, and that was exactly what was happening to me.

Upper Walker Elementary School also shows inclusion to their ESL students by highlighting the fact that each one of them come from different backgrounds. Rather than having the ESL students feel embarrassed that they don't know how to speak English that well because they were born and raised in a different country, the faculty at that school always find ways to have ESL students embrace their culture and identity. One way the school goes about this is by putting on an international day for ESL students to present information about where they are from and what they love about their country/culture. The project itself is not only personal and fun for the students to work on, but it is also very educational because it teaches them how to write paragraphs about certain aspects of their country (e.g. food, clothes, history). It also teaches them how to present to an audience and allows them to practice reading over and over again. In a way, the students feel more empowered than the teacher/tutors because it is about their country, and they are the master of a subject for once. It is not something the teacher can tell them what is right or wrong, instead they are able to navigate freely as it is a topic they know better than anyone. This empowerment is sometimes important to students because, instead of feeling like the teachers/tutors are the ones that know everything, it is finally in their hands to talk about something they know a lot more about than the teachers/tutors. Seeing them and helping them throughout their project made me realize how important it is to take a step back from always trying to teach them about American society and instead ask them to teach us about their culture.

Helping my students with this project made me wish I had the opportunity to do this project when I was little. I think it would have helped me build my self-confidence because I would try to hide my true identity for the longest time. By identity I mean where I was from, what religion I was, and how I looked. I remember throughout all my elementary school years, I would try to become as Americanized as possible. That meant I would refuse to take my mom's homemade Egyptian dishes for lunch because it looked and smelled "weird." I remember the one time I convinced myself that it was not a big deal for me to take my mom's food to school, a white girl named Julie made fun of what I was eating. She sat there with her peanut butter and jelly sandwich while I sat there with my rice, lamb, and eggplant dish. I remember I felt so embarrassed because after Julie said, "Ew! What is that?" she proceeded to get up and move to the other table because of the smell. From that day I refused all my mom's offers and just ate bagels and cream cheese.

I also had trouble facing my true religion and expressing it for a long time. I did not start wearing my hijab until sixth grade, so all the years prior to that, I would deny that I was Muslim because there was no physical appearance that said otherwise. Growing up in America during the post-9/11 era made it really difficult to want to claim my religion. Although I knew that Islam was not the reason why 9/11 happened and that that event can only be blamed on terrorists not a religion, saying I was Muslim had a negative connotation that I hated. Little Mariam did not want to be labeled as a terrorist, so I tried my hardest to cover up that I was Muslim. I remember during book fairs we were required to bring a parent so that they would pay for the things we wanted from the bookfair. I never wanted my mom to come with me because she wore the hijab and that would just blow my cover. Instead, I would beg for my dad to come because he looked like a regular middle-aged guy with no one specific religion attached to him. To little Mariam, saying that I was Muslim was going to get me bullied because I thought the world hated us.

Another part of my identity that I tried to hide was my natural features. For example, I went to a predominantly white school and so many of the students had straight hair. As a child, I always had very puffy thick hair. I hated it so much because I did not think it was pretty since it was not straight. I remember telling my mom to straighten my hair every other day because I could just not go to school with my hair being all puffy like a ball of hair. There were many other physical features that I was insecure about because I was comparing myself to the white students who spoke perfect English and seemed to not have struggles outside of school. Since none of my teachers or school staff showed interest in the diverse background of their students and how unique everyone is, it made me feel like my culture/identity was not worth sharing. I felt like no one really wanted to know about who I truly was, and for that reason I wanted to push away my identity. I wanted to be like the majority, like every white student so that I could fit in and not be seen as this immigrant student who has "weird" hair, "weird" food, and associates herself with a terrorist religion. That's why I want to emphasize the importance of asking about and being interested in your ESL students' backgrounds. As a former ESL student, I can promise you that we do not find it rude that you ask us questions about our culture/religion. It actually makes us feel important and unique in the sense that we get to talk about our cultural identity that differs from someone else's cultural background.

Back in Brooklyn, there was an ESL final examination at the end of each year to see whether or not a student was ready to be out on their own and leave the ESL program. Every year, that day was my least favorite day. It was a day full of anxiety, stress, and fear of failing. I failed my ESL test my first year, and my second year, but now it was my third time taking it. I wanted nothing more than to pass because I just wanted my recess time back and to not be excluded anymore. I remember waking up an hour earlier than usual to get a good breakfast in, to turn on the TV and watch the Disney channel to get me excited for my least favorite day, and to pray a little more to God to help me pass my ESL exam. I really did not want to fail again. I remember getting dressed which was when my stomach started to hurt because I was getting very anxious. I was walking alongside my mom in silence on the way to school because the exam was the only thing on my mind. The bell rang for recess and all my classmates were happy and joyful, but there I was feeling dreadful and scared of what was to come. The usual routine happened—my ESL teacher came and took me to the most depressing room, white walls and no pictures. I sat on the squeaky chair with a packet and a freshly sharpened pencil in front of me. Before I picked up the pencil, I said a quick prayer, begging God one last time to help me pass. I proceeded to pick up the pencil, wrote my name on the first page, and then flipped the page to start my exam. The first question had a picture of *arybia*.

First question: "What is this picture of?"

I knew it. It was *arybia* in Arabic, but what was it in English? I could not recall right then, so I went to the next question.

Second question: "The car drove past the big tree. Which one shows a picture of a tree?"

Easy. Tree is *shagrah*. I circled the tree with no hesitation. I re-read that statement though and realized that *arybia* mentioned in the question before was the car. I felt like I had just solved a Rubik's cube. I went back to the first question and wrote "car" for the answer. I felt more confident in the exam as the first two questions gave me hope that maybe I did have a chance at passing. I went through question by question until I was done. I got up and turned in my exam to my teacher, and then I went back to the classroom.

A couple days passed by until I got pulled out of the classroom by my ESL teacher. I was confused though because the recess bell did not ring yet.

"Am I in trouble?" I asked my teacher.

She did a short fake laugh and said, "No, silly. You passed your ESL exam!"

I was above cloud nine. I tuned out everything that came out of her mouth after that and just had a smile big enough to show all my teeth. I was freed, or at least thought I was.

What I failed to see the day I passed my ESL exam was that although the school system does not consider me an ESL student anymore, I will never reach the level of mastering English like a native speaker. Fourteen years later and I still see myself putting in double the effort to get the same grade as a native speaker would. It may not look like it because I work hard, but I still struggle with reading, writing, and speaking English. The funny thing about being a multilingual student is that in America, my English feels like it's below average because there are a lot of words I don't understand or even know how to say. However, when I go back home to Egypt, my English is seen as the most perfect English one could speak. The reality of all this is that I will always be an ESL student, even when I am an ESL tutor because learning English is a never-ending process.

As my journey of learning English continues, I plan on using what I have learned through my experience of being an ESL student and tutor to become the most effective speech pathologist I can be. Being a speech pathologist, in my opinion, is very similar to a tutor because essentially it will be a client and I practicing how to say a phrase, read a book, and develop communication strategies. I will be taking my advice mentioned in this paper—such as giving students breaks, not pushing them beyond their boundaries, and being mindful of personal issues the student is facing—when dealing with clients. Essentially, my clients are like the ESL students, and I am the speech pathologist/ESL tutor.

Just like in tutoring ESL students, one of the most important things is to build that tutor-tutee friendship. I really want to take the friendship that I never had with my ESL teacher and turn it into a positive bond with my clients. I will be using similar strategies of forming that friendship I made with my ESL students, which include asking them about their background, trying to relate to them in some form, and finding unique ways to make each session fun rather than making education dreadful. I am speaking back to the world about my miseducation through the form of speech pathology as I will help clients be able to communicate effectively, but I'm also sharing my story to inspire people to have a more inclusive approach to life.

My story is not just for ESL tutors, educators, or speech therapists—it's for every person who encounters others with a different background/identity, whether that is religious, cultural, racial, or gender. At the core of each profession is human interaction, and as times are changing and society is progressing towards a more inclusive environment, every individual needs to reflect on their day-to-day interactions and how inclusive/welcoming they are. Throughout my reflection on my ESL experiences, I came up with strategies on how to approach ESL learning; however, it is through my experiences that I realized that the main change that needs to happen is within oneself and one's willingness to learn about multi-cultures, religions, different identities, etc. Working towards having a well-rounded knowledge and continuously being open-minded, in my opinion, will allow for human interactions to feel like that tutor-tutee friendship I had where I was able to learn from them, about them, and make them feel valued for who they are as I was actively listening. I share my story so that others' stories can be heard.

WORKS CITED

"Asian/Asian American Scholarship in Rhetoric and Composition: Risks and Rewards." Conference on College Composition and Communication. Tampa Marriott Waterside, Tampa, FL, 19 March 2015. Sponsored by the Asian/Asian American Caucus.

Cooper, Marilyn M. and Gail Y. Okawa. "From the Editor." *College Composition and Communication* 53.3 (2002): 393–95. Print.

Hoang, Haivan V. "Campus Racial Politics and a 'Rhetoric of Injury.'" *College Composition and Communication* 61.1 (2009): W385–W408. Print.

Lu, Min-Zhan. "Professing Multiculturalism: The Politics of Style in the Contact Zone." *College Composition and Communication* 45.4 (1994): 442–58. Print.

—. "Redefining the Literate Self: The Politics of Critical Affirmation." *College Composition and Communication* 51.2 (1999): 172–94. Print.

—. "An Essay on the Work of Composition: Composing English Against the Order of Fast Capitalism." *College Composition and Communication* 56.1 (2004): 16–50. Print.

Lu, Min-Zhan and Elizabeth Robertson. "Review: Life Writing as Social Acts." *College Composition and Communication* 51.1 (1999):119–31. Print.

Mao, LuMing. "Rhetorical Borderlands: Chinese American Rhetoric in the Making." *College Composition and Communication* 56.3 (2005): 426–69. Print.

Monberg, Terese Guinsatao, and K. Hyoejin Yoon. "Ruptures, Wounds, Possibilities: Asian/Asian American Disciplinary History and Scholarship." Conference on College Composition and Communication. JW Marriott, Indianapolis, IN, 20 March 2014. Sponsored by the Asian/Asian American Caucus.

Sciachitano, Marian M. "Introduction: Feminist Sophistics Pedagogy Group." *College Composition and Communication* 43.3 (1992): 297-300. Print.

Shen, Fan. "The Classroom and the Wider Culture: Identity as a Key to Learning English Composition." *College Composition and Communication* 40.4 (December 1989): 459–66. Print.

Swearingen, C. Jan & LuMing Mao, eds. CCC Special Symposium on

East–West Comparative Rhetorical Studies. *College Composition and Communication* 60.4 (June 2009): W99–W106. Web.

Wu, Hui. "Writing and Teaching behind Barbed Wire: An Exiled Composition Class in a Japanese–American Internment Camp." *College Composition and Communication* 59.2 (2007): 233–58. Print.

You, Xiaoye. "Ideology, Textbooks, and the Rhetoric of Production in China." *College Composition and Communication* 56.4: 632–53. Print.

Young, Morris. *Minor Re/Visions: Asian American Literacy Narratives as a Rhetoric of Citizenship.* Carbondale: Southern Illinois UP, 2004. Print.

Mariam Mohamed is a 4th year student at the University of Virginia who was born in Cairo, Egypt. She immigrated to the U.S. at five-years-old. She likes to spend her time aiding others, whether that is tutoring at local schools or working at the student disability center at UVA to academically support those who are blind/visually impaired.

CHAPTER FIVE

When in the Workplace: A Consideration of Hair

Deborah Wood

By the time that I was four-years-old, my mother and I had become accustomed to a long-standing ritual—Wash Day. At the time, it was a dreadful one. Every week, I would prepare for Wash Day by wailing on the cold kitchen floor or hiding in my closet as my mother called me to embrace what would soon lead me to beg for my last breath. Wash Day. It consisted of shampooing my hair in the bathtub, stretching my hair with a blow dryer, and then styling my hair with barrettes or "beadies" (as I had called them). It seems all too simple, but it was not. Because every week, my mother would unravel my hair from the previous week, implore a jet stream of water that often worked quite well on my face rather than its target—my scalp and hair—blast heat that was all too warm for my little neck, and tug harshly on my hair to pack it into a neatly-roped twists. Every week, I felt the pain of a thousand ancestors reminding me of my origins. My hair. The hair that caused me torment. I questioned why my hair would frizz and shrink and need heat. I pondered whether the other girls—with hair unlike mine—felt damaged not by the physical pain but the emotional pain of Wash Day. But then, we met her. The woman who would never remove the pain of Wash Day but would make it more bearable with magic goop—a white pasty substance that I would later refer to as a relaxer.

I had never experienced anything more unusual than magic goop. No doubt, I still remember having water gush down into my little eyes. But with this special woman, Wash Day became "wash day." There was no heat on my neck from the blow dryer nor a need to tug my hair and mask the pain with barrettes. Once the magic goop (the relaxer) was put on for as long as this woman wanted and rinsed out with extra care, my wash day would end with a new type of tugging. Two tongs with immense heat crushed each section of my strands of hair until I no longer pondered about whether my hair was unlike the other girls. I did not question my difference anymore. Likewise, magic goop only needed application no less than one month assuming I did not "sweat it out," as this woman told my mother. It was amazing. It was amazing until it was not.

By the time I was 8, magic goop had gone from being my savior to my captor. I hated it. I missed Wash Day. My hair, the hair that my mother had raised alongside myself all those years, was leaving me. But it did not make sense. I was not old enough to lose my hair. I was not sick enough to have it fall out. Moreover, magic goop did not target the root of my scalp but the ends. Like yarn being cut from a ball, my ends were being gnawed at by magic goop. My emotional pain surged just as it had before, as I now doted on why the other girls were gaining hair gradually and cutting their hair deliberately while my hair was leaving me rapidly and non-consensually.

My mother, having noticed the change in me, felt pain, too. All she had wanted to do was spare me from Wash Day, to make me feel better. And she would do it again by ridding me of magic goop. In fact, my mother and I left the woman one day only for her to tell me that we should go see another woman. She was Ms. Y and my hair had actually spent the better half of my adolescence under the care of Ms. Y, having both the nurturing heart of my mother and the sorcery of the woman with magic goop. Over the years, I still had wash day with Ms. Y, but I was content with it. Of course, that all changed when I resisted the urge to wake up early in the mornings every Saturday to have her do my hair. I wanted the freedom to sleep in. And more importantly, I wanted the freedom of wearing my own hair.

When I was 13, I stopped going to Ms. Y (as dearly loved as she was). I reclaimed Wash Day for myself, now becoming its sole conductor. Since my hair had been straightened from the plates of the flat iron for nearly five years, it was effectively damaged. It was during this time that I realized something. I removed all beliefs of my hair that I had ingrained in me and approached my hair by its root, literally. I began to see my hair as bushy rather than frizzy. I saw the shrink as a sign of healthiness. If my hair springs up—as it naturally does, then surely it was in good shape. The next year, I cut most of my hair off. All of the damaged pieces that remained limp after being hit with water were gone. I felt new. I had officially had my hair. Wash Day was cut too. No blow dry. No heat. No tools of agony. No women. Just a girl. Myself. And sadly, the looks. I went to school with short hair, short hair shaped like an afro.

Even while I began both freshman and sophomore year in a high school with girls whom I
thought would have hair like myself, I was truly alone. I could not transport myself to the *Black Is Beautiful* era of the 70's and chant "Black Power!" in veneration of my hair. I could not because each stare reminded me of the present that I had to face. And for better or worse, I had to grow something more than my hair. I had to keep away from the damage to my self-esteem. And with time, I did just that. As my hair grew, my perspective grew also. Until one night, I just blurted it out. "I am natural," I told myself. "I am natural." It was a reclamation like no other. I desperately wanted others like myself— Black girls and women—to experience it. That is until I realized that my hair, like many other real or perceived attributes about myself that constitute Blackness, is scrutinized in the workplace.

Workplace discrimination is described as the unfair treatment of an employee or job candidate based on age, disability, sex, religion, color, pregnancy status, national origin, and/or race. More specifically, racial workplace discrimination manifests through various means, extending as early on as biased hiring practices through the course of employment. Numerous studies have highlighted the disparity in hiring based on "racial" characteristics, such as names as well as hair. Before Black people can enter the workplace, they are often met with discrimination based on their names. A study conducted involved randomly assigning "white-sounding" names (such as Emily Walsh) to half of a fictitious group of job applicants and "Black-sounding" names (like Jamal Jones) to the other half, with various levels of quality in the applicants' resumes. Researchers found that there was a 50% increase in call-back rate for white-sounding applicants such that for every 10 "white" applicants' resumes and for every 15 "Black" applicants' resumes, there was a single callback. Likewise, a higher quality resume for a "white" applicant produced a 30% increase in call-back rate over a lower quality resume for a "white" applicant while there was a statistically insignificant difference in the disparity between the call-back rates for the "Black" applicants' resumes across quality level (Bertrand and Mullainathan). For a real pool of applicants, the result of this study implies that Black people, by way of their names, are unfavorably looked upon when selecting candidates for interviews regardless of background.

Of course, if Black people do receive call-backs, they still must contest with the interview process which requires them to be face-to-face with a set of interviewers. This inevitably means that physical traits can be used to discriminate against Black interviewees. That is, the story of the Black applicant who sounds all too perfect on paper walking into the interview or job only to have her offer promptly rescinded is no less than a glaring possibility. This is especially so when it comes to "Black hair." Our hair, due to the distinct styles adopted like afros, braids, and twists, can affect Black people's outcomes when it comes to job interviews. In particular, Black women with natural hair are seen as less professional, less competent, and less likely to be recommended for a job interview than Black women with straightened hairstyles and white women with either curly or straight hairstyles (Koval and Rosette). Yet when I first went natural, I never envisioned that my undamaged hair would be used against me. Nothing about my ability to do math or even carry a conversation changed drastically after I cut off my damaged hair. And surely if I had undergone the process of applying harsh skin-lightening cream and stopped using it in the name of my health, I would be rewarded for such efforts. But, yet again, this just illustrates that despite possessing the qualifications for particular jobs, Black people are discriminated against during the hiring process. Yet the discrimination does not always end there.

Discrimination on the basis of race occurs *in* the workplace, too. This discrimination is typically seen with hurling derogatory remarks or racial slurs and displaying racially offensive symbols. And it can be uttered by a coworker, supervisor, or customer. The Equal Employment Opportunity Commission, or EEOC, is a federal agency that enforces Title VII of the Civil Rights Act of 1964, which makes it unlawful to discriminate in hiring, discharge, promotion, referral, and other facets of employment, on the basis of color, race, religion, sex, or national origin. In the 2019 fiscal year, roughly 33% of the 72,675 charges of workplace discrimination the EEOC received incorporated racial discrimination but charges of racial discrimination had a reasonable cause in only 490 charges (1.9% of the 23,976 race-based charges) according to the EEOC (Race-Based Charges). If a passive agency like the EEOC alone does not deter or stop racial discrimination, then active non-profit organizations like the NAACP and SPLC can also step in if they see fit. Yet this does not address the crux of the issue. Racial discrimination in the hiring process and the workplace are perpetuated largely by people, and stopping it falls on the backs of not only the people involved, but also the businesses, bureaucracy, and media that encourage the behavior by allowing said HR managers, coworkers, supervisors, and clients to continue to perpetuate this discrimination. Businesses that do not set an example of the people who represent their institutions, the bureaucracy that provides loans, grants, and tax-cuts to these same businesses when needed, and the media that encourages people to exercise beliefs in racial stereotypes and beliefs, are all responsible for exhorting racial discrimination in the workplace.

Now, I do not want nor expect non-Black people to walk on eggshells when it comes to hiring. Nor do I want non-Black people to avoid the unfair treatment of Black people in the workplace by highlighting the extensive network that it takes to uphold racial discrimination in the workplace. However, what I will be clear of is that racism negatively affects business, period. A study by Citigroup showed that the US economy, as a whole, lost $16 trillion dollars due to racism, in part due to discouraging Black entrepreneurs but also due to disparities in wages between Black and white workers among other causes (Akala). Still another study by McKinsey and Company showed that closing the racial wealth gap between Black and white people could increase the GDP by 4-6% by 2028, a development that would positively affect all Americans, even white and other non-Black minorities ("Racism Is Hurting"). Add on the negative mental effects of experiencing racism, and the productivity of Black workers may go down due to resulting poor mental health, which surely is not good for business.

And, like a stubborn child who does not listen, businesses should not be rewarded with government aid if they are known for practicing racism. From Google, a company that has been in the news more than one time as a result of intersectional racial and sexual discrimination of Black women, to Wells Fargo, a company whose Chief Executive Charles Scharf claimed that there is simply too small of a talented pool of Black applicants for them to hire, there is a history of bad behavior for some businesses that is exhorted when the bureaucracy lets it slide by providing them with monetary aid. And it should not be done, as ingrained as it may be.

Even if the bureaucracy decides to "reward" businesses infamous for racial discrimination, there is no reason that media cannot effectively be targeted. In fact, diverse media like the Academy-Award winning short film "Hair Love" is a perfect example of the change that can be made to alter racial workplace discrimination. "Hair Love" weaves both overarching cultural attributes like the journey that comes with nurturing natural hair—as was the case in my own life and many like the daughter in the film and myself, as well as individualistic attributes like the mother's cancer diagnosis that acts as the catalyst for the father doing his daughter's hair. This combination of elements allows the film to extend far enough to avoid Black racial stereotypes and likely explains some of the reasoning as to why the film is linked to legislation passed less than a year ago in my home state of Virginia to ban hair discrimination under the CROWN Act (Hamedy). It especially appeals to a subset of Black people who are actively advocating for positive representation. Even if you cannot create an award-winning film, I have found that the simplest thing that you can do is to avoid media that paints "Blackness" negatively. Neutral or positive media are both productive, with the latter generally being best. As well, your local news describing the crime committed by an individual who happens to be Black is one thing (just a reflection of a single person's acts), but a movie like *Jumanji*, wherein Jack Black's impersonation of the notably Black character Fridge (originally played by Ser'Darius Blain) curses more than Blain's rendition ever did, is another. It signals stereotypes at play, so just be mindful. And to make it even easier, adopt the slogan "just be mindful" when you encounter these situations. When you see it, say it, and it will stick. "Just be mindful." And yes, you can hashtag it, too.

WORKS CITED

Akala, Adedayo. "Cost Of Racism: U.S. Economy Lost $16 Trillion Because Of Discrimination, Bank Says." NPR, *NPR*, 23 Sept. 2020, www.npr.org/sections/live-updates-protests-for-racial-justice/2020/09/23/916022472/cost-of-racism-u-s-economy-lost-16-trillion-because-of-discrimination-bank-says.

Bertrand, Marianne and Sendhil Mullainathan. "Are Emily and Greg More Employable than Lakisha and Jamal? A Field Experiment on Labor Market Discrimination." *The American Economic Review*, vol. 94, no. 4, 2004, pp. 991–1013. *JSTOR*, www.jstor.org/stable/3592802.

Hamedy, Saba. "It's Official: Virginia Is Now the Fourth State to Ban Hair Discrimination." *CNN*, Cable News Network, 5 Mar. 2020, www.cnn.com/2020/03/05/us/virginia-ban-hair-discrimination-bill-trnd/index.html.

Koval, Christy Zhou, and Ashleigh Shelby Rosette. "The Natural Hair Bias in Job Recruitment." *Social Psychological and Personality Science*, Aug. 2020, doi:10.1177/1948550620937937.

"Race-Based Charges (Charges filed with EEOC) FY 1997 - FY 2019." *U.S. Equal Employment Opportunity Commission*, https://www.eeoc.gov/statistics/race-based-charges-charges-filed-eeoc-fy-1997-fy-2020.

"Racism Is Hurting the Economic Well-Being of the US and Its Workforce - Including White Workers." The Kinder Institute for Urban Research, kinder.rice.edu/urbanedge/2020/08/03/racism-economics-hurting-american-gdp-and-prosperity-white-people.

Deborah is a fourth-year biomedical engineering student at UVA. To create this piece, she took the life lessons, experiences, and suggestions of family, strangers, as well as herself. This piece embodies a recollection of the misjustice that arises with politicizing and discriminating against Black women and girls' hair.

CHAPTER SIX

Finding Pluralism through Polyrhythm

Madaline Marland

Jazz music is proof that time is circular, not linear, as some of the scientific faith may choose to believe. Tempestuous undercurrents carried polyrhythms across the Atlantic. Unfamiliar beat structures braided with the structure of the New World. Hymnals and work songs grew from the backs of enslaved peoples, and, when they died, decomposed and gave life to ragtime and blues. Louis Armstrong and John Coltrane were born in soil already saturated in history, and their thoughts were reconstructed in swing and its baby, Duke Ellington. Bebop, Afro-Cubanism, funk—they are all reincarnations, waves in a tidal being that was never born and will never die.

The moon is supposedly the gravitational force behind tidal changes, and on some nights it wakes me from a dead sleep, gasping for air and hands I will never touch. I sit upright with a startling sense of displacement-

From stretch music, a note:

if I stretch far enough, can I reach the edges of our diaspora? I am omnivorous!

...

My eyelids, dampened by the dew of dreaming, dry into a wide set stance of white-hot desperation. In my moments of craving, jazz soothes my shaky withdrawal.

Delirium's caustic, metallic tang softens on my tongue within the first few sounds. Notes of syncopation replace it: paprika, cayenne, cinnamon bark, and hot chili pepper. From the dimly lit corner of a 1940's club comes the prickled wailing of a lonely saxophone. Brazilian psychedelia melts into Qatari soul and London-produced slicks. In scrolling, long feeds of album covers show portraits of men and women and children living under tonal harmonies labeled unnatural by the classical world. Behind their cheeks are African-born talking drums. Their eyebrows have the wild splay of brush mallets, held in the calloused hand of a slouched cat riding the back of the beat. Her unconcerned tssss-ts-ts-tssss marries with background static, characteristic of poor audio quality, until one is not able to be discerned from the other. The chilled shadows of indistinguishable ride cymbal rhythms quench the cultural dynamism and vibrancy of earlier riffs; finally, I am awakened.

Madaline Marland is a chemical engineering and music student at the University of Virginia. Her work is driven from love for Science Lady, a version of herself ten years in the future who wears red lipstick and a lab coat. Native to Baltimore, she takes current residence in the trails and laboratory spaces of Charlottesville, Virginia.

CHAPTER SEVEN

Diversity & Inclusion Efforts: A Foundation, Not a Solution

Hana Qureshi

I always knew what phrases such as *misrepresentation* and *discrimination* stood for but fortunately didn't know what it meant to experience them. With the changing and extreme political climate that has arisen in recent years, I have now experienced some of these coined phrases. I have been personally burned by the dangerous narrative of hatred that our current politicians spout from their throne of privilege. The pride for country that I'm supposed to hold has been corrupted by fear of the "other," a dangerous public rhetoric. It is public representation through the power of mis-labeling. It instills fear in many individuals simply because they don't know what the "other" means. It causes abuse and violent acts. It can be seen in the rise in police brutality against black people and the substantial increase of anti-Asian hate crimes since the pandemic. It can be felt by individual bodies.

I am Mexican, Muslim, and a daughter of two immigrants. I have been called a terrorist. I have been told I am the reason why the country is deteriorating. That it's my fault for jumping the border, bringing violence and drugs. I've been looked at strangely in stores and have been followed around. I have been asked insensitive questions and have been terrified to walk the streets by myself out of fear that I'll be assaulted. I've been told to stop speaking Spanish because "this is America." When faced with these racist and hurtful instances, my reaction at times did not reflect maturity and did not absolve the perpetrator of their initial misconceptions. I would yell, performing my rage in a spectacularly loud and obtrusive manner, and in the end, most likely pushed these individuals closer to their incorrect labels of me. In responding with anger, I further perpetuated the very stereotypes I was attempting to combat. Now when these instances occur, I calmly try to show them my perspective while being careful not to insult or demean them. Unfortunately, at times this doesn't pull them to my side, but it does manage to defuse powder-keg situations.

But these individual acts of defense aren't a solution to the dangerous rhetoric of the "other." They are a temporary band-aid for an illness that is kept alive by the very heart of our societal institutions. At the root of all these current issues lies the U.S. government. The institution that should help move us towards a solution is led by a majority of individuals who do not experience them. As a result, many institutions are turning to diversity and inclusion programming (D&I) in the workplace. Indeed, D&I programs are an example of a small step in the right direction. In an ideal world, diversity and representation would be a given in public institutions. There wouldn't be a need to address something as an example of "representation." Individuals would be valued for the ideas they can provide, whether that is based on professional experience or demographic background, both seen as valid criteria. Communities would feel represented in all the institutions that they take part in.

While this growing D&I movement does provide some benefits, expecting institutional change from such efforts, although ideal, is naïve. More accurately, I would argue minorities have been tasked with the challenge of pushing for big steps in the right direction and settling for small ones, such as D&I. Creating institutional change requires a deeper analysis, both in governmental as well as conceptual institutions. Is diversity for the sake of "diversity" really progress? Are quotas, Affirmative Action, and blind resumé readings necessary, but imperfect, solutions? How can we create explicit results for an implicit occurrence? What is the definition of diversity? Do labels limit an individual's nature, their unique intersectionality? These are the questions that I believe *can* drive change on a small and large scale, but I believe D&I programs in academia and the professional business world is flawed.

I have worked with start-ups that aim to connect minorities with professional opportunities and I have participated in diversity and inclusion programs. These programs need to be analyzed through a more critical lens. The existence of D&I efforts doesn't mean that a problem has disappeared; if anything, these programs sometimes can incite more issues. For example, such programs may connect minorities with opportunities, but what good are those opportunities if individuals aren't prepared with the right resources and tools to succeed and prosper? Those who are at a disadvantage because of their demographic should also be given access to the tools to succeed. As such, the majority of these diversity and inclusion programs only scratch the surface of their equitable mission.

In addition, as someone who has been selected and participated in such programs, there always exists the looming question of "Am I here because I am valued for more than my demographic? Or do I just fill a diversity spot?" I have no issue filling a diversity spot because my main drive is to succeed and get to the top through any means within an unbalanced system. I understand, however, that these spots can serve to devalue some individuals. In addition, diversity and inclusion programs tend to phrase the term "diversity" as an issue, further alienating any of us who fall into that category. Diversity and inclusion efforts are littered with negative messages and words, including implied threats, further pushing those who hold misconceptions into their ideology.

The idea that bias can be outlawed or that these discussions or solutions are black and white is another potential flaw in such efforts. According to Harvard Business Review, the "three most popular interventions make firms less diverse, not more, because managers resist strong-arming." Studies also show that voluntary training leads to better results than obligatory training which can result in resistance and anger in the workplace. In D&I programs, we are seen as labels, not as people with ideas. Yet, it is *these* ideas are what are important for diversity in the workplace. Ideas that stem from different backgrounds and experiences define what it means to be diverse, not simply the color of your skin or your economic status. So how can a solution be found? The answer is by restructuring our current institutions that hold up and preserve the power imbalances in our society: businesses, the media, government, and education.

Businesses and corporations have already begun to increase these measures. Although their efforts should be appreciated, they do need to be improved for better results. This benefits social corporations' reputations, such as B-corps, and will keep employees and clients pleased. Encouraging but not forcing D&I training, acknowledging and responding to employee differences and complaints, and making an effort to increase participation from every employee on every level are ways businesses can produce effective efforts. The media holds two fronts concerning diversity and inclusion. There is an abundance of POC and minority media figures that aren't given opportunities. In addition, the narrative encouraged by the media influences how people see minorities, so making sure this narrative is positive rather than harmful, but also holds institutions and individuals accountable, is important. Government institutions have a huge influence on communities. As such, leadership should reflect the voices of those represented. Many laws are disenfranchising to communities of color, whether that be zoning issues or voting restrictions, an analysis on how each law can and will affect these communities should be enacted to minimize the damage. Finally, educational institutions should be upfront and teach about these efforts while also enacting them, allowing students to learn and become active leaders. Exposing children from an early age to respect and identify differences can foster different experiences as well as also point out similarities. Such efforts will help develop future citizens who are more conscious of the POC experience. Restructuring institutions is a costly, time-consuming, and difficult task but as soon as we start to accept that we have an imperfect solution, the sooner we can attempt to arrive at a more suitable one.

Although I just listed out specific ways each institution can begin restructuring, representation is one overarching potential solution that is essential for a sustainable restructuring. Representation of various ideas, backgrounds, races, religions, sexualities, nationalities, cultures, and experiences is critical and necessary. Without it, any small step towards the right direction won't be able to evolve into anything significant, but is representation for the sake of representation the same as diversity for the sake of diversity? The answer to this lies in the position and utility of that representation. Where are these diverse individuals being represented? Is it only within diversity pamphlets and propaganda, or is it in impactful government roles, higher education positions, C-suite executive boards, and blockbuster movies? Until diverse ideas and the people behind them can penetrate the high strata of those who drive society, we will be stuck on cruise control our whole lives, taking a backseat while these institutions never put their foot on the gas or take action to move our society forward faster. D&I efforts have placed diverse individuals in these institutions and have helped move us forward, now it's time to push more and demand more.

The first step to all of this is representation, but how to achieve representation would require a much longer and separate analysis. For now, we have certified that *identifying* a problem doesn't *solve* a problem. For this reason, D&I efforts are lacking effectiveness and creating more issues. We also demonstrated that while individuals can chip away at the issue and provide small steps, a systemic change in our institutions needs to occur so that minorities can stop having to settle for less within their own society. And we proposed on possible solution to systematically change our institution. Representation, which has the effect of multiplying and elevating platforms for minorities to create change. I recognize that this proposed solution has issues, I have had to face these issues within my own participation in representational programs. But the fact of the matter is we can't expect to change our institutions if we aren't even a part of them in the first place. Once we can participate and become the catalyst of our own change, we can start tackling all the remaining issues. Diversity and inclusion efforts are a foundation, not a solution. Representation may be our current solution but will be our future foundation.

WORKS CITED

Williams, Joan C. et al. "Why Diversity Programs Fail." *Harvard Business Review*, 14 Sept. 2020, hbr.org/2016/07/why-diversity-programs-fail.

Hana Zavala Qureshi is a Commerce student at the University of Virginia. She writes, "What best defines my identity, passions, and activities is intersectionality. I love to dip my toes in a variety of subjects, seeing how they connect and how that connection can create impact."

CHAPTER EIGHT

Inequity & Healthcare Algorithms: Novel Budding, Dangerous, but Resolvable

Wamia Said

The Tuskegee Syphilis Experiment: where what was supposed to be a six-month observational study became four decades of intentional withholding of treatment for the sake of observing the progression of untreated syphilis in hundreds of unsuspecting African American men. The Flint Water Crisis: where the negligence of far too many public health officials resulted in the lead poisoning of thousands of Flint's low-income residents. The ongoing COVID-19 Pandemic: where Black and Hispanic Americans are infected at rates disproportionate to their share of the population.

For years, the American healthcare system has failed its minority populations. Without a proper understanding and acknowledgement of the underlying systemic issues that have allowed these injustices to prevail, we will be forced to sit complacently as we watch healthcare inequity evolve and amplify with the rise of technology dependence in medicine.

With major advances in technology, it is no surprise that predictive algorithms and artificial intelligence have become essential tools in assessing the needs of patients—from identifying high risk patients that will receive benefits from extra care programs to informing diagnoses of cardiovascular disease. In their most basic form, these algorithms accept data and exploit pattern recognition to make predictions based on their accepted data. Though powerful, algorithms make assumptions to generate these predictions and these assumptions—rooted in our larger systemic failures as a society—have consequences that we cannot afford to ignore.

In a study published by Science Magazine, researchers found that a widely used healthcare algorithm inaccurately predicted the health risk level of African American patients time and time again. This discrepancy can be attributed to the fact that the algorithm assumed an individual's health-related spending was correlated with the amount of care that the individual necessitated. When researchers analyzed patient data using active chronic conditions, the percentage of African American patients who were identified as "high risk" increased substantially (Obermeyer et al) Whether it's the fact that majority-minority residential areas often lack an adequate access to healthcare providers or that insufficient access to transportation often deters individuals from seeking the care they need, the inequities faced by African Americans that forces them to, on average, spend less on healthcare than their white counterparts are erased by this algorithm's assumptions (Taylor)

In addition to these assumptions, the accuracy of an algorithm is heavily dependent on the training data fed to it. For example, training data is often obtained from the population's internet usage and, as a result, big data has become a culprit of perpetuating inequity through what is now known as "digital redlining"—where minority groups are excluded from training datasets solely due to their lack of internet access and usage (Cahan) This becomes especially dangerous when it comes to healthcare algorithms—as Dr. Khullar puts it, "if [the training] data doesn't include enough patients from a particular background, it won't be as reliable for them." After stepping on and neglecting its minority population throughout history, the American healthcare system will be faced with nothing less than an amplification of its existing issues if proper caution is not taken in choosing algorithmic training data sets.

Though the situation is alarming, it is important to note that algorithms have only recently begun to be incorporated into healthcare—in other words, it is not too late to rectify this inequity before we are forced to witness more of the dreadful ramifications of our inaction. The remedy for this injustice, however, must be a collective effort from the institutions that have given these algorithms the power and leeway to perpetuate this discrimination. It is by coalescing the power of: the algorithm manufacturers that have recklessly built these biased algorithms; the medical institutions that have disregarded the needs of their African American patients far too many times; the educational institutions that have omitted the history of medical racism from general curriculum; and the general public who has yet to be informed on the magnitude of this issue that we will begin to combat this new era of medical racism. Together, we can and will build a future of equitable healthcare algorithms that prove accurate regardless of racial background.

Algorithm manufacturers are, quite obviously, integral to this movement. In contrast to the Tuskegee Syphilis Experiment, the inequity that has resulted from healthcare algorithms was not intentional—rather, it was only the result of trekking through the uncharted waters of new technology. Data scientists have always been loyal to the data, not to their algorithm—now that we have uncovered the harm these algorithms have, it is the moral obligation of our data scientists to tweak their algorithms accordingly. Additionally, internal issues with the field of data science are responsible for allowing these discriminatory algorithms to endure past preliminary planning. Referring back to the Obermeyer et al study, it is seemingly harmless to use "annual health spending" as an algorithm's training data until the disparities in healthcare access across races are brought up as a confounding variable. These conversations are more likely to occur with input from a diverse group of data scientists but given that underrepresented minorities make up only 13.3% of engineers and scientists in the US, this is often not the case (Allen-Ramdial). Given our long history of medical discrimination, it is crucial that algorithm manufacturing companies commit to diversifying their staff and instilling adaptive attitudes in their data scientists. Without these reforms, we cannot expect to maintain the integrity of our healthcare algorithms and we will ultimately exacerbate the injustices we have already witnessed.

The involvement of medical facilities as well as medical schools is also critical. Medical facilities make the conscious choice to employ the algorithms they employ; as a result, they must begin to implement strict vetting procedures for these algorithms and require mandatory check-ins to ensure the algorithm maintains integrity. These check-ins, however, will never be successful unless their staff has the knowledge and experience with algorithms to identify issues when they occur—this is where the role of medical schools comes in. With technology quickly advancing and making its swift entrance into the medical field, it is urgent and essential that medical schools modify their curriculum accordingly. Moreover, medical schools must also begin to comprehensively integrate the history of medical racism in their curriculum so that students can better understand and identify the more subtle instances of medical discrimination, such as those encountered in healthcare algorithms. Given that the Hippocratic oath—*primum non nocere*, do no harm—is embedded into every doctors' morals and that these reforms promote this principle by ensuring equity for all patients, it is reasonable to trust that medical institutions will be eager in driving these transitions.

All of these reforms begin with the people. Unfortunately, this issue and the topic of medical racism in general is one that does not get enough attention in the media. As a result, it is imperative to launch informational campaigns to raise awareness for these issues. In order for these campaigns to be as effective as possible, the issues must be presented in such a way that ties the consequences back to each individual. For example, this could be achieved by designing an interactive and accessible online resource that allows users to input statistics about themselves and receive feedback on the stark differences in the care they would receive if their race, gender, or socioeconomic background were any different. By informing the general public, we are able to spark engagement and discussion regarding this lesser-known issue. This newfound support from the public could then indirectly bring in support from existing activist groups that work toward broader goals of equity and justice. These partnerships could act as a catalyst to propel protesting and lobbying efforts that would pull algorithm manufacturers, medical facilities, and medical schools toward the movement.

As technology advances, discrimination and the ways discrimination can be perpetuated advances as well. With this in mind, it is important for us to acknowledge these issues as they are revealed to us—not once it is too late. Recently, there have been several strides forward to amend these injustices. Senator Cory Booker (D-NJ) and Senator Ron Wyden (D-OR) called for the Federal Trade Commission and several healthcare companies to increase transparency in their tactics for combatting discrimination in healthcare algorithms ("Booker, Wyden Demand"); the AAMC and HHMI laid out their vision of future competency requirements for doctors, including the "integration of data, modeling, computation [...] and informatics tools" as one of their goals (Keeley); Obermeyer et al ended their paper by describing their collaborative efforts with the manufacturers of the algorithm they studied to reframe the algorithm to be more equitable.

Our healthcare system has failed underrepresented minorities far too many times. As data scientists, as doctors, as humans, it is our duty to fight for these rights—we cannot and will not be complacent any longer. These small victories prove that, regardless of our past, this will not be our future.

This is a chance for us to redeem and reclaim the American healthcare system as *ours* with the help of equitable algorithms, but it begins with the support of our algorithm manufacturers, our medical institutions, and, most importantly, you.

WORKS CITED

Allen-Ramdial, Stacy-Ann A. and Andrew G. Campbell. "Reimagining the Pipeline: Advancing STEM Diversity, Persistence, and Success." *OUP Academic*, Oxford University Press, 24 May 2014, academic.oup.com/bioscience/article/64/7/612/2754151?login=true.

"Booker, Wyden Demand Answers on Biased Health Care Algorithms." *U.S. Senator Cory Booker of New Jersey*, 3 Dec. 2019, www.booker.senate.gov/news/press/booker-wyden-demand-answers-on-biased-health-care-algorithms.

Buolamwini, Joy and Timnit Gebru. "Gender Shades: Intersectional Accuracy Disparities in Commercial Gender Classification." *Proceedings of Machine Learning Research Conference on Fairness, Accountability, and Transparency*, 2018, pp. 1-15, http://proceedings.mlr.press/v81/buolamwini18a/buolamwini18a.pdf.

Cahan, Eli M. et al. "Putting the Data before the Algorithm in Big Data Addressing Personalized Healthcare." *Nature News*, Nature Publishing Group, 19 Aug. 2019, www.nature.com/articles/s41746-019-0157-2.

Keeley, Jim. "AAMC/HHMI Committee Defines Scientific Competencies for Future Physicians." Howard Hughes Medical Institute, 4 June 2009, www.hhmi.org/news/aamc -hhmi-committee-defines-scientific-competencies-future-physicians.

Khullar, Dhruv. "A.I. Could Worsen Health Disparities." *The New York Times*, The New York Times, 31 Jan. 2019, www.nytimes.com/2019/01/31/opinion/ai-bias-healthcare.html.

Obermeyer, Ziad et al. "Dissecting Racial Bias in an Algorithm Used to Manage the Health of Populations." *Science Magazine*,

American Association for the Advancement of Science, 25 Oct. 2019, science.sciencemag.org/content/366/6464/447.

Taylor, Jamila. "Racism, Inequality, and Health Care for African Americans." *The Century Foundation*, 19 Dec. 2019, tcf.org/content/report/racism-inequality-health-care-african-americans.

CHAPTER NINE

The Vision of Tomorrow in Healthcare

Shannon Deavers

As an assistant in a chiropractic clinic, I get to not only witness but experience healthcare. Unlike many healthcare workers, I am grateful to be at a clinic which eagerly welcomes people of all different backgrounds without making them fear for their comfort, rights, or lives. Female Muslim patients come to my chiropractic clinic despite the touch restrictions their religious beliefs often require. After realizing the time and care we give them during their appointments, Hispanic parents bring their children in for treatment. In these cases and more, patients were treated with equal respect, no matter their native language or religion; they are welcomed into a stable environment and made comfortable. By viewing health as a human right and prioritizing the development of a secure patient-doctor relationship, this clinic treats a diverse array of patients who confide in our care. Unfortunately, there are numerous medical clinics that are unable to say this and instead reinforce the widespread discrimination present in our nation's healthcare system.

According to the Agency for Healthcare Research and Quality (AHRQ), studies in 2019 revealed that "For about 40% of quality measures, Blacks (82 of 202) and American Indians and Alaska Natives (47 of 116) received worse care than Whites. For more than one-third of quality measures, Hispanics (61 of 177) received worse care than Whites." These communities, along with Asian Americans, are being disproportionately affected by the systemic inequality in our healthcare system. While these statistics don't get into the nitty gritty details of what "worse care" looks like, it doesn't matter. All medical professionals take an oath to treat all patients equally, and yet the official numbers from the yearly Congress-mandated National Healthcare Quality Report (NHQR) and publicized first-hand experiences of these marginalized populations deem this an act of perjury.

This inequality of care of ethnic and racial minority groups is something far more serious than the majority believes. Simply having brown or black skin, or speaking partial English versus full English, makes these people much more vulnerable to medical mistreatment. After observing hospitals across the nation, one study unveiled the despicable truth behind these disparities in healthcare: "Patients with limited English proficiency were more likely to be harmed than their English-proficient counterparts when they experienced adverse events" (Shepard). As gruesome as it sounds, this heightened risk of deliberate harm from medical professionals is a reality for many minority groups in our country. Though discrimination and racism are knowingly ingrained in our society, the ramifications these minority groups endure is far less talked about, let alone acted upon. It's not just about unequal access to education or affordable housing; in healthcare, it could surely be about life or death.

Furthermore, the lack of cultural competence by physicians–the ability of healthcare systems to care for patients of diverse cultural, social, and linguistic needs–too often results in them utilizing cultural stereotypes. An Institute of Medicine study provided clear examples of such occurrences. In the report, a Hispanic physician, speaking on behalf of his colleagues made it clear that "Healthcare providers make assumptions about their patients based on race or ethnicity" (Institute of Medicine). A Hispanic patient spoke to about a specific encounter with a healthcare provider, saying, "'There's a lack of acknowledging the person and making one feel welcome. All of the courtesies that go with the profession that they are paid to do are kind of put aside. They think they can get away with a lot because 'Here's another dumb Mexican'" (Institute of Medicine). This failure to first acknowledge then address cultural barriers–whether it be language, religious belief, etc.–leads to not only a lack of respect and confidence in the patient-doctor relationship but an understandable sense of fear in the thoughts of these minority groups.

While one can argue that these physicians operate in an inherently racist system and that everyone–including those in the field of healthcare–is susceptible to implicit bias, there is no excuse for these medical professionals to not make an effort to enact change. To combat this overt racism and discrimination in healthcare, both patients and physicians need to recognize, name, and understand the actions and attitudes that reside in this bigotry. Dr. Altaf Saadi, a general academic neurologist at Massachusetts General Hospital (MGH) and an instructor of neurology at Harvard Medical School, asserts this idea. She argues that "We—as physicians and society more generally—must realize that the struggles of one marginalized community are struggles of all of us. My fight as a Muslim-American doctor to serve my patients without fear of racism, and the fight of an African American patient to be treated with dignity and respect, should also be your fights" (Tello).

Each and every person can play a role in this fight to uphold this vision and progress towards change. The very first step is to assume that most people are apathetic, disinterested, unmotivated, or downright hostile when it comes to the blatant racism, white privilege, and mistreatment of individuals rampant in our nation's healthcare system. While this will make the process trickier, it's a vital element to acknowledge. The next step might be creating a community health outreach program. Such a program would be used to dispel the fear of minority groups and reassure patients that there are physicians who they can entrust with their care. Here, gathering the physicians able to carry out such a program is obviously crucial. Weighing the costs and benefits of both the community health outreach program and those who oppose the program's core beliefs comes next. More specifically, it would be beneficial to think about how exactly these outreach programs would work given the circumstances during a pandemic. After compiling these rudimentary ideas, it's necessary to develop an organized detailed instruction guide on how to execute this outreach program from start to finish, providing a solid foundation to achieve this vision.

From my personal experience as a healthcare worker, I have found it inspiring to watch this vision of tomorrow come to fruition in the clinic. While our nation's healthcare system seems to be designed to deny, not support, the right to health, I have discovered how medical professionals can still shift this perspective by treating those less privileged and those of various backgrounds equitably. If each person could create opportunities for small victories like the ones my chiropractic office has made, this vision of tomorrow so many of us are hoping to achieve would become reality. To achieve this vision, however, we must remember that it's important for everyone to do their part.

WORKS CITED

"2019 National Healthcare Quality and Disparities Report." *Agency for Healthcare Research and Quality*, Dec. 2020, https://www.ahrq.gov/sites/default/files/wysiwyg/research/findings/nhqrdr/2019qdr-final es.pdf.

Institute of Medicine. *Unequal Treatment: Confronting Racial and Ethnic Disparities in Health Care.* Eds. Brian D. Smedley, Adrienne Y. Stitch, and Alan R. Nelson. Washington, DC: The National Academies Press, 2003, https://doi.org/10.17226/12875

Shepard, Susan. "Challenges of Cultural Diversity in Healthcare: Protect Your Patients and Yourself." *The Doctors Company*, 19 Dec. 2019, https://www.thedoctors.com/articles/challenges-of-cultural-diversity-in-healthcare-protect-your-patientsand-yourself/

Tello, Monique. "Racism and Discrimination in Health Care: Providers and Patients." *Harvard Health Publishing*, Harvard Medical School, 16 Jan. 2017, https://www.health.harvard.edu/blog/racism-discrimination-health-care-providers-patients-2017011611015. Accessed 9 July 2020.

Shannon Deavers, who wrote this essay during her first year at UVA, worked as a chiropractor's assistant school and aspires to become a chiropractor in the future. Outside of work, she loves to bake, lift, hike, and play soccer.

CHAPTER TEN

An Unseen Human Rights Violation

Ida Sampson

I want a Black doctor. I want a female Black doctor. I want a doctor who looks like me, talks in my vernacular, and is equipped with basic listening skills. I also want safe and effective healthcare. All of these statements are related, and all of them should be attainable. I want Black women to become a priority within healthcare instead of a casualty.

The healthcare system is flawed. A more accurate assessment would be to describe the healthcare system as corrupt. This is an observation, not an interpretation. While claims of disproportionate care provided to minority communities can be dismissed in the abstract, the reality is that Black women are 2-6 times more likely to die during childbirth than their white counterparts (Flanders 1), 2-3 times more likely to die from preventable heart disease and strokes (Huerto 1), and are 60% less likely to be prescribed pain medications by an ER physician (Janakiram 2). While the factual discrepancies in the standard of care are of value as an interpretive framework, they often provide an opportunity to escape the simple fact that Black women are dying. Yet there seems to be little urgency on finding a solution. So again, I state that I would like a Black doctor.

I am not remiss to the reality that merely having an African American physician will not solve racial disparities within the field of healthcare. But it couldn't hurt. A month ago, I sat in a UVA hospital, unable to breathe, scared but knowing that I would be fine because

I was in the hospital. There were hundreds of individuals floating around in white coats that would extend the Hippocratic Oath to me. "How long ago did the asthma attack start? When did you first experience symptoms? Around what time did you begin coughing?" Similar questions spaced out appropriately inhibiting my overstimulated brain from noticing their repetitive nature. They are being thorough, ensuring an accurate history is being recorded. "This is normal. You're fine. The pain will go away." Words of comfort were provided instead of a treatment plan. Alternative questioning began. "Do you have a primary care physician? Are you able to afford outside care? Here is a reference to a free clinic." Four hours later, it was revealed that my lungs were inflamed, and I needed to see a specialist immediately. I was not fine. The pain did not go away. I was not helped. I was sent away.

Failure of the interrogative techniques applied to obtaining a patient's history is not inherently a racial inequity but rather a medical practice error. One that could be resolved by alteration to the medical school curriculum. Perhaps a Black doctor would have made the same error. While I am hesitant to speak only in the realm of probability, I do maintain that if I was given the opportunity to speak to a Black doctor, I would have been better equipped to give a more accurate depiction of my medical history. The luxuries of comfort and the ability to relax around physicians are not necessarily ones that are shared across minority or cultural lines. While it seems to be lacking in value in comparison to access to diagnostic tests, a hospitable doctor patient relationship is equal in its importance.

The healthcare system within the United States has a long-standing history of abuse against the female Black body. In an 1858 Medical Journal, a doctor cited assessing the profitability of Black bodies as being one of the primary duties of southern doctors (Owens 1). Further abuse was endured by Black bodies following their deaths in which their remains were utilized as learning tools for future white medical students. Medical fields also served as a vessel of support for political actions such as the legalization of chattel slavery with childbearing capabilities being at the forefront of the movement. Doctors were utilized to determine possible sources of infertility as well as aid enslaved midwives in cases of difficult labor. Despite attempts to prevent infant death, approximately 50% of infants born to enslaved

Black women were stillborn or died before the age of one (Owens2). Pioneering procedures, such as cesarean and surgical techniques to repair fistulas, were achieved through experimentation on enslaved African women, often without the provision of anesthetic (Owens 2).

Post-slavery relations between African American women and health-care systems are merely a continuation of earlier patterns. Black women continue to be 3-4 times more likely to suffer pregnancy-re-lated issues than their white counterparts (Owens 3). Additionally, the mortality rate of Black infants is 2.3 times higher than that of non-Hispanic white infants (Owens 3). Within Charlottesville out of 1,000 births, 26.3 black infants experienced death before reaching the age of one compared to the 2.6 deaths experienced by white in-fants representing the highest rate of infant death held in the com-monwealth of Virginia (ABCDMAG 2). Medical ailments that Black women are often predisposed to, such as hypertension and eclamp-sia, have been psychologically and genetically linked to stress caused by living in a racist society (Owens 3). More practical issues, such as the inability to obtain an accurate family history, are correlated to the side effects of slavery disrupting familial lineages. Concepts of racial inferiority first utilized in slavery have translated into the racial discrimination that limits the quality and type of healthcare African American women are able to access today.

Assumptions that medical practitioners are able to give equivalent treatment to all patients is reliant on the idea that the relationship be-tween all individuals and healthcare is uniform. Lack of uniformity in the amount of trust held within the healthcare system due to histori-cal interactions results in discrepancies in the amount of information even the most well-intentioned doctors are able to achieve. In other words, without a proper history, a doctor cannot be held responsible for an inability to acquire the appropriate diagnostic test. I concede that my main argument rests on a massive assumption that all back doctors share the same cultural experience as their Black patients. However, our current form of healthcare relies on the assumption that all medical practitioners are equipped with the ability to under-stand the cultural significance and perspective of each of their pa-tients. So I wonder, could the proposal of Black patients with Black doctors, even though it relies on the assumption of a universal expe-rience, be a possible upgrade from the current circumstances?

Healthcare is inherently a business, a vehicle of the capitalist enterprise that is the heart of the United States. An individual's socioeconomic status is directly linked to the quality of care provided. Due to de facto segregation, the correlation between race, financial standing, and access to vital services is undeniable. The basic laws of economics ruled by capitalism, namely resource allocation and efficiency in resource utilization, directly apply to health disparities.

As such, in order to provoke change there must be a threat to the economic sector of healthcare. The government is the main supplier of funds for public hospitals. Whereas private organizations obtain funding from a wide array of intermediaries (ranging from insurance companies to donors), considering the more centralized sources of funds seen in public institutions they are an easier target. Target public officials, particularly those who serve as members of committees dedicated to allocations of funds. With most of these being local institutions, there is a small degree of separation between them and their constituency. Identify the amount of Black female support as well as allies to the cause who contributed to their elections through the use of petitions insisting that they place new requirements outlined by the movement or reduce funding to hospitals and medical practices failing African American women. Failure to impose these requirements would result in removal of support for future reelection.

Proposed requirements should include an increase in preventative screening of diseases that disproportionately affect the Black community, particularly Black women; strict guidelines established to ensure that the standard of care is extending to all individuals; reforms in the way malpractice suits are handled limiting the level economic elitism held within previous systems; and increased data collection on the mortality and morbidity rates of the African American patients. Instead of complete depletion of funds upon failure to adhere to suggested requirements, insist on the reallocation of funds to institutions such as free clinics or other hospitals which have a lower discrepancy in patient care among racial lines.

This is not just a social or political issue that only pertains to individuals that directly face its injustice. Racial disparities embedded within healthcare are affecting everyone's pocketbook. There are approximately 5.7 million African Americans who use Medicare (National Committee to Preserve Social Security and Medicare 1). Congruently, it is estimated that up to $15.6 billion a year could be saved by the Medicare program if health related racial disparities were eliminated (Center for Medicare Advocacy 2). Additionally, the reduction of preventable diseases, such as diabetes and hypertension to similar rates seen in white populations, would cut $23.9 billion in healthcare costs (Center for Medicare Advocacy 2). In an NEBR study, it was shown that Black men who were seen by a Black doctor were 47% more likely to take a diabetes screening test and 72% more likely to receive a cholesterol test than those who were seen by a white doctor (Torres 3). Therefore, individuals who lack a significant point of relation to the cause, but just would like their taxes to be reduced or put to better use, may want to consider petitioning their local governments to levy more rigorous requirements on public hospitals. In other words, implementing strategies to reduce racial disparities would greatly help the government's budget and yours.

I recognize the privilege of being able to critique the healthcare system—a privilege that was not extended to the African Slaves whose bodies were used by the father of gynecology to make groundbreaking discoveries; a privilege that was not held by Henrietta Lacks when her DNA was used without her consent to expand the world of medical research exhibiting the historical abuse of the female black body that informs the present maternal health crisis; a privilege that was not given to Kira Dixon, Dr.Shalon, Yoland Kadima, Amber Rose, Tatia Oden, and so many more who were unable to tell their story of failed medical ethics due to death during childbirth. But it is also a privilege held by my ability to access healthcare, however flawed it may be. Changes cannot be made by activists who are comfortably held in a safe space that is academia. Furthermore, to rectify racial disparities held within the healthcare system, the reach cannot be limited to the providers and individuals who function within its infrastructure. Besides reforms to the currently adopted insurance system, which prevents many from seeking any form of healthcare let alone specialization, we also need to promote conversations between doctors and patients of every background on what they need to feel comfortable. Action cannot be taken if doctors are not cognizant of the areas in which they are failing.

Finally, there need to be efforts to increase the level of communication within Black families and communities concerned about health. Open dialogue about family history disrupting the stigmatization around discussing pain, dispelling the idea that Black women are unlimited vessels of strength unable to describe the pain that they feel, and abandonment of ideas that Black women's pain is manageable and acceptable needs to occur. People need to acknowledge that is, in fact, a human rights violation, not just a small flaw in medical procedure, but a threat to notions of equality and safety that are espoused and protected by our democracy. Black women have been failed from the conception of the constitution with their lives being deemed less than and their stories irrelevant. This inadequacy in recognition is continued by the maltreatment of Black women in the current healthcare system. The healthcare system needs to exhibit that they recognize the irrefutable fact that Black women's lives matter.

WORKS CITED

ABCDMAG. "Infant Mortality and Race." *ABCD Magazine*, Word-Press, 11 Mar. 2019, abcdmag.com/2019/03/11/infant-mortality-and-race-examining-health-disparities-in-charlottesville-past-and-present/.

Flanders-Stepans, Mary Beth. "Alarming Racial Differences in Maternal Mortality." *The Journal of Perinatal Education*, U.S. National Library of Medicine, 2000, www.ncbi.nlm.nih.gov/pmc/articles/PMC1595019/.

Huerto, Ryan. "Minority Patients Benefit From Having Minority Doctors, But That's a Hard Match to Make." *M Health Lab*, University of Michigan, 31 Mar. 2020, labblog.uofmhealth.org/rounds/minority-patients-benefit-from-having-minority-doctors-but-thats-a-hard-match-to-make-0.

Janakiram, Chandrashekar, et al. "Sex and Race or Ethnicity Disparities in Opioid Prescriptions for Dental Diagnoses Among Patients Receiving Medicaid." *The Journal of the American Dental Association*, vol. 150, no. 10, 2019, Https://Jada.ada.org/Article/S0002-8177(19)30441-6/Pdf.

"Medicare and Medicaid Are Important to African Americans." *NCPSSM*, National Committee to Preserve Social Security and Medicare, 29 June 2020, www.ncpssm.org/documents/medicare-policy-papers/medicare-medicaid-important-african-americans/.

Owens, Deirdre Cooper and Sharla M. Fett. "Black Maternal and Infant Health: Historical Legacies of Slavery." *American Journal of Public Health*, American Public Health Association, Oct. 2019, www.ncbi.nlm.nih.gov/pmc/articles/PMC6727302/.

"Racial and Ethnic Health Care Disparities." Center for Medicare Advocacy, 27 July 2017, medicareadvocacy.org/medicare-info/health-care-disparities/.

Torres, Nicole. "Research: Having a Black Doctor Led Black Men to Receive More-Effective Care." *Harvard Business Review*, 10 Aug. 2018, hbr.org/2018/08/research-having-a-black-doctor-led-black-men-to-receive-more-effective-care.

Ida Sampson is a third-year majoring in medical anthropology in the college of Arts and Sciences at the University of Virginia. As a pre-med student, she aspires to a career which will incorporate the discipline of anthropology to address the health disparities within the medical field. Through research as well as internship opportunities, she has explored the issue of increased maternal and fetal mortality among black populations.

CHAPTER ELEVEN

A Hopeful Imagination

Andrea Villar

As a second-generation immigrant, it became apparent to me at an early age that my abundant life had all to do with the decision my parents made to leave Peru to come to the United States. It was not easy for them, but they managed to make careers for themselves and have three children that would be their greatest and most prideful fruits of their labor. At an early age, I knew I wasn't going to have the most expensive boots in my class, nor have my mother become a "room parent" volunteering at the class parties. Yet, I was fully aware that I was always going to come home to a loving, supportive, and strong-willed family. Our money struggles taught me resourcefulness; my first job at the age of fifteen taught me about hard work and grit, my mother's struggle to speak English taught me patience, and the ample success my siblings and I have had taught me to be not only grateful but to be willing to help those that are not as blessed as I am.

My anger started when Donald Trump was elected President of the United States and implemented a "zero-tolerance" policy through an Executive Order, an order intended to upsurge the criminal prosecution of those entering the United States illegally. It was soon after that news outlets began to report how undocumented immigrant parents traveling with their children were being prosecuted and separated from their children. Children were being ripped out of the arms of their parents. These children were scared, alone, and suffering under the inhumane conditions of the ICE detention centers. On the news, I saw pictures of children packed into the small rooms with aluminum blankets and mothers wailing as the ICE officers tore their children apart from them. Our country was proceeding, as always, with such malicious acts of oppression. I could not dare spend a single moment without this on my mind. My anger amplified as I imagined myself and my family in their shoes, cold and mistreated.

Then, last semester, I was completing a research paper on the stigmatization of illegality. As I was going through Trump's past speeches regarding immigration, I became aware of the fact that the media is one of those institutions culpable for the distribution of his malicious oratory. In one speech in 2015, he voiced, "They're bringing drugs. They're bringing crime. They're rapists" (Trump 2015). I asked myself: Are they rapists, or are they the ones working on the fields, under the scorching sun, picking vegetables for you to eat? Are they criminals, or are they washing dishes in the restaurants you eat at? Are they illegal, or are they simply looking to escape the poverty and violence of their mother countries? As these thoughts rushed through my brain, feelings of compassion and empathy began to overcome me. It was clear to me at that moment that these anti-immigrant politicians and their constituents were lacking just that: empathy. They were lacking the ability to imagine themselves in the shoes of those immigrant children being yanked away from their parents and prosecuted under the law, alone and afraid. This was when I realized that immigration was what caused my heart and mind to sting. The socially constructed idea of illegality enraged me further, and from then on, I was going to be an advocate for a more humanitarian approach to the issue on immigration.

As a student at the University of Virginia, I have had the privilege to learn from some of the most gifted people on topics on social issues. Being a part of organizations such as *UNDOC UVA* and the *Latinx Student Alliance* have provided me and the other members with the opportunity to become more informed and active regarding issues affecting marginalized communities, such as the Latinx individuals at UVA and in Charlottesville. We are already on a steady path, but we must continue. We must reform the immigration legislation that permits such callous treatment of unauthorized immigrants entering the United States. Specifically, ensure that *Immigration Customs Enforcement* and *Customs Border Protection* authorities abide by certain standards and are held accountable for inhumane treatment. In addition to this, my goal is to improve the process in which immigrants are deemed legal and documented. It is imperative, however, that this fight be a form of civil disobedience. If there is anger, there needs to be a longing for a better country, not violence. Though my judgment on figures such as Donald Trump have heightened my vexation regarding this issue, I do not intend to attack him personally, but rather to challenge him and those pillars that support this unjust form of operation.

And we must use the very media tools that have cultivated anti-immigrant rhetoric to support pro—immigrant policies by encouraging the empathy and compassion needed for change. The first step to complete this will be to demonstrate the horrors occurring at the border through social media and other news outlets. This will ignite the illustrative and imaginative factor necessary for the empathy that will ignite reform. Politicians and other Americans need to imagine themselves crossing the border and in the ICE detention centers. How can this be done? Though it would be a challenge for some, traveling to the Mexico-Texas border to provide first-hand evidence of the abusive occurrences would be an effective power in fighting for immigrant representation. From there, creating a social media campaign will not only raise money for this movement, but encourage other Americans to join this good fight. Furthermore, this united movement can contact Congressional representatives and demand that they defund ICE and create a pathway to citizenship for the millions of undocumented immigrants in the United States. These measures are in no way intended to be a full plan of action for the reformation of immigration policy, but the first steps for a hopeful revolution through civil disobedience.

As humans, we are taught that anger is bad. We are taught to control the fire within us, to throw water on it, and move on. I challenge that belief. Perhaps the answer to the social and humanitarian issues in America -- and the world, essentially - lies within what makes us mad. I believe it is necessary to take what outrages us and turn it into, if not social change, then a humble gesture for someone in need.
Now, as I sit here, venting about my outrage regarding the inhumanity occurring at the border, I remain hopeful for change. I am irate, I am upset, I am worried, but I am hopeful. I realize that it is not only in my power, but in the power of every student at UVA to stimulate change in the United States, the country in which my parents and

many others sacrificed plenty to become a member.

To any individual doubtful of their influence on the policies in America and to the students at UVA that feel as though they have lost hope for a better future, I urge them to find the will and energy to embark on a journey for social change, to join us in working for immigrant equality and justice in our country. Without the will, without the passion, and without the hope for a future of change and justice, one does not exist. A brighter future exists if we can imagine it. And remember ,there is no prerequisite to be an activist -- if you have an eagerness to be a part of the change, that is the only requirement.

Andrea Villar is currently a first-generation Latina student at the University of Virginia studying English and Sociology. This is Andrea's first published piece of writing and when she is not writing for social justice or stuck in a book, she loves spending time with her loved ones, her dog, Ruqa, and eating Peruvian food!

CHAPTER TWELVE

Infiltrating the Pillars of Inequality in Immigration

Emily Gaw

Since the dawn of time, humans have immigrated in search of better opportunities. Neither you nor I would be here without immigration. My ideal world would be borderless and leaderless. In our current political society, is that even possible? Perhaps, but given human nature, it is highly unlikely. A more realistic vision would be a world with more open borders and equal opportunity, where all humans have the right to move and work where they choose. Today, a lack of official paperwork can render an immigrant powerless and subject to abuse. To begin a journey towards that ideal society, the U.S. government could widen immigration channels and reallocate money from border control to foreign aid. Opposing these goals, however, is a substantial group of Americans who believe that those who immigrate illegally are threatening their own livelihood and their sense of a "patriotic" America. This group supports politicians who pass laws infringing on the very basic human right to work in order to deter immigration in the first place. We need to find a pathway forward that respects the rights of all humans, undocumented immigrants and citizens alike. With this essay, I hope to provide one such possible pathway.

At the heart of the matter, the right to immigrate for a better life is a human issue. Crossing the 1954 milelong U.S.-Mexican border illegally is a dangerous endeavor; over 10,000 people have died during the crossing over the last thirty years ("Migrant Deaths," "Mexico-United States Border). For many in Central and South America, the U.S. is associated with economic opportunity, potential for education, and most importantly, personal safety. Channels for legal immigration to the U.S. are narrow, and many simply do not have the familial connections, work authorization, or asylum status to be granted legal immigration. Even for those trying to immigrate legally, the wait is forbidding. In 2020, the immigration waiting list from Mexico was over 1.2 million ("Annual Report). Crossing the border illegally, for many South Americans, is their only chance.

Very few illegal immigrants come forward with stories of crossing, thus the horrors facing those illegally residing in the U.S. remain mostly hidden. One such woman, Mireya, is now legally a U.S. citizen and has come forward with her story. Mireya crossed the southern border three times. She was 15 the first time she fled Mexico. In fleeing, she was attempting to avoid a family member who had been molesting her since she was 11. During her first attempt, she was duped by the *coyote* (person helping her cross) into sexual slavery and taken to a house where she was raped repeatedly. Eventually, she escaped and made it across the border with the help of a kind border patrol officer. After being deported for the first time, Mireya attempted a second crossing. This time, she was forced to hold her breath while crossing a river underwater and barely made it, suffering an asthma attack. Other members of her group were ripped away by the river's currents. The leaders of the group told her to wait there for a specific call while they returned with others crossing the border, but they never returned: "We waited and waited and waited, but that call never came. It was just the noise of the water" (Courteau). Those who perished in the waters that night and on other nights are not counted in the official death toll.

But even the perilous crossing is not necessarily the most difficult facet of immigrating illegally. Once inside the U.S., undocumented immigrants live in constant fear of deportation, the result of which is limited economic and social mobility. In 2019, ICE deported an average of 733 people per day ("ERO FY 2019 Achievements"). The fear of leaving one's children alone without saying goodbye is enough to make undocumented workers accept workplace abuse, injustice, or maltreatment without a word.

I remember clearly the moment I became aware of this injustice. In 2007 I turned seven, and my father lost his job. In 2013 he found a new one, and we moved from New York City to Virginia in time to celebrate my twelfth birthday and begin sixth grade. In New York, I perceived myself as less wealthy than my peers, a fact that I didn't actively try to conceal but simply didn't mention. Somewhere in my 12-year-old brain, I had gotten the incorrect impression that there was something less appealing, less trustworthy, and less gracious about being poor.

The weekend before I started sixth grade, my parents and I went to Staples to purchase purple binders. As we approached the parking lot, I saw a group of men loitering about the entrance. They seemed to be eyeing our car. As we entered the lot, they chased after our car. Initially, I was terrified. But after my father rolled down his window to speak to them, they dispersed. He pulled in, and turned around to see me, frozen in the backseat. He told me these men were undocumented and in search of work. It took me a few minutes to fully understand. When we emerged from Staples and I slid into our backseat, clutching my purple binders, the men were still there. Suddenly, I didn't feel poor. Unemployment of the kind my father had experienced seemed a privilege. From my child-like vantage point, I became aware of real poverty as well as a poverty of hope that stemmed from a lack of opportunity. We arrived home, and I almost cried; I couldn't put it into words, but I was saddened at our society that gave these men no option but to undertake these humiliating (and dangerous) lengths to find work.

As I grew older, wiser, and more educated, I started to grow out of my childhood ignorance and became more aware of the prevalence of the struggles of undocumented and those held down by the very nature of society - those with nowhere to turn.

I began to follow the news and heard stories of those like Luis Zavala, a 45-year-old undocumented construction worker from Louisiana who had complained to his employer about less-than-fair wages. When his employer asked him and his fellow workers to gather to receive pay raises, ICE showed up, dragged him and his fellow workers outside, and handcuffed them: "They came very aggressively, with their guns pointed. They threw me on the floor. They put their foot on my back. It was very terrifying" (Harris).

Still, the immigrants whose stories are heard and published are only the tip of the iceberg. Workers who speak on dangerously inhuman conditions, low wages, and workplace discrimination among other topics are threatened with unemployment at best and deportation at worst. This unspoken rule keeps undocumented immigrants at the bottom of the socioeconomic ladder. Antonio Lozano, a documented immigrant working construction in Texas, speaks on the effort put in to sustain a family: "Sometimes you don't go home. You just get ready for the next shift. We work for our families. That's the main reason. We have bills to pay and families to support." Lozano's boss had refused to pay him and his fellow workers (mostly undocumented) for their work, and Lozano took a stance. Shortly after, they began to receive threatening text messages including, "I am going to do whatever it takes to have them sent back to Mexico."

Geographically, immigrants who cross the southern border tend to find jobs wherever they can, whether farming on the west coast, in inner cities, or elsewhere. This said, because of the fear associated with revealing their identity, the leaders of movements must be naturalized citizens. The focus of these movement to fight for undocumented immigrants' rights should target audiences most likely to support the cause. In this case, it is imperative that the movement focuses on supporters in progressive districts & states with large Hispanic, African American, Asian, and recent immigrant populations. This means states with large urban populations, like California and New York.

What opposes this movement towards basic human rights? Long story short, the rights of undocumented immigrants have been cast as a social issue and manipulated into a partisan and racial issue. In what must be the bottom pit of human decency, President Trump told Americans that undocumented immigrants from Mexico are "criminals, drug dealers, and rapists" (Lee). Other Republicans argue that the general motivation behind the politicization of the rights of undocumented immigrants is economic: Studies have demonstrated that undocumented immigrants have a net drain on society's resources (Camarota). By reducing rights for undocumented people, politicians hope to make the U.S. a less attractive destination so fewer will immigrate illegally. While on the surface the economic evidence is valid, human rights and decency should always triumph over economics. How should we measure the value of a human life? Of human happiness? Politicians whose actions place economics over human issues would undoubtedly have a different perspective if their own family were at risk. However, the hardships facing undocumented immigrants are far removed from the average American's daily life.

Many forget that, like any human would, immigrants *chose* their best option by immigrating. Despite knowing the incredibly stressful, unjust, and difficult nature of undocumented life in the U.S., not to mention the risk of death while crossing, thousands still *choose* to cross every year. This speaks louder than any statistic. It is our responsibility to rise to the occasion to help those desperate for basic subsistence and freedom rather than falling into the shortsightedness of bigotry and greed. How should we go about tackling a sociopolitical issue? We must first examine what institutions are causing the issue and how open they are to change.

The first obvious institution perpetuating the current immigration crisis is the U.S. government, which is supported by the aforementioned people with anti-immigrant biases. With the support of the government, discriminatory laws are put in place and funds are directed towards persecuting undocumented immigrants. Since the government is a representative of the people, let me define the two "sides" of this issue: the current anti-immigration Republican party and the non-profit or grassroots organizations promoting rights for undocumented immigrants. Both groups have sway over the government and its associated institutions, and therefore have the potential to affect change. The U.S. government's concept of legality is integral to the definition of "illegal immigration." The U.S. has passed many discriminatory laws against undocumented immigrants. A clear lack of preventative measures regarding unjust treatment of undocumented immigrants is a reflection of the politicization of local, state, and national courts. It's important to note that beneficial laws have also been passed: DACA, DREAM Act, etc. At its core, however, U.S. Law remains the basis for deportation, the fear of which enables unscrupulous businesses to abuse undocumented workers. One particular federal law, the *Immigration Reform and Control Act of 1986* (IRCA), actively keeps undocumented workers from working legally by requiring employers to check the legal status of their potential hire. Overturning this law is the first key to gaining basic human rights for undocumented immigrants.

Courts have enforced this law, punishing the employers of undocumented workers with up to ten years in prison and hefty fines ("When Breaking"). While the IRCA has some provisions to protect basic workers' rights, it is insufficient. Employers who are willing to hire in violation of the law are often unafraid to alert ICE and deport any workers who complain about unfair wages or working conditions (Campbell). As a result, many endure subpar conditions and abuse in order to provide for their families. This legal structure is powerful in blocking economic and social mobility for undocumented workers and slowing immigration. The number of apprehensions at the southern border has fallen from 1.2 million in 1985 (the year before the IRCA) to 0.85 million in 2019 (United States Border Patrol). Another government structure, albeit relatively immovable but crucial in our analysis, is ICE. Under President Trump, funds were increasingly channeled into ICE, an agency whose primary goal is to deport illegal immigrants. Many of ICE's tactics are, simply put, a horrific abuse of human rights. When businesses around the U.S. shut down in March, due to COVID-19, ICE's crowded detention centers remained open and continued processing people. 21 people have died in custody in 2020 alone (Nowrasteh). As a democratic representation of Americans, the U.S. government has potential to be swayed in the direction of the majority opinion. This opens the stage for the grassroots movement I mentioned earlier.

A second integral institution complicit in the issue is U.S. businesses. Currently, businesses are split into two camps: those willing to hire undocumented workers and those unwilling. The first set of businesses are mostly manual labor factories and farms who are willing to take the risk in exchange for the ease of hiring these workers. Many of these businesses abuse their workers, paying extremely low wages and placing them in unsanitary working conditions, knowing the workers are too afraid of the consequences of lawsuits to take action. The second group of businesses unwilling to risk hiring undocumented immigrants are either afraid of the legal consequences via the IRCA, morally opposed to it, or don't need the predominantly unskilled workers. Very rarely do businesses speak for the rights of undocumented workers, often for fear of being singled out by ICE or being labeled "unpatriotic." At the end of the day, the U.S. has a free market economy. All businesses that want to thrive will hire the cheapest least risky workers. With the removal of the IRCA, this could be widened to include undocumented workers.

A third institution—media—has great potential to sway the minds of the U.S. population towards supporting political parties that advocate for the rights of undocumented immigrants. Unfortunately, media sources today are so polarized that citizens can easily choose to watch news that is skewed only towards their political bias. Similar to democratic governing, the media responds to the demands of the people. Whatever garners them the largest watcher base will also make them the most money. Ultimately, it is a little more complicated, with the media accepting "donations" to cover up issues or directly publicize other issues. For instance, the Republican party uses its media platforms to convince voters that only their party's vision can save the nation by, in part, "selling" the oppression of undocumented immigrants disguised as self-preservation. The psychological concept of Maslow's hierarchy of needs explains that humans must meet their basic needs before meeting higher needs. By casting undocumented immigrants as a threat to Americans' jobs and safety, Republicans instill fear in voters with this threat to the most fundamental level of the hierarchy. This has proven extremely effective, and legislators have been able to pass numerous laws aimed at reducing illegal immigration.(I should note that both major political parties, Democratic and Republican, are guilty of promoting anti-immigrant bias. This is why I have not included the Democratic party on the side of the grassroots organizations).

A side effect of the dramatization of modern media platforms is the warping of many voters' minds when undocumented immigrants are portrayed as evil and threatening. This propaganda has horrific consequences. In a more drastic example, a gunman in Texas opened fire in Walmart, killing 22 and injuring countless others. In a manifesto he published before the slaughter, he warned of an "Hispanic Invasion" of Texas and claimed that he was simply "defending my country from cultural and ethnic replacement brought on by an invasion" (Panetta). The words "replacement" and "invasion" have been repeatedly used by conservative media when referring to immigration.

Representing the opposite side of this issue are the non-profits, community, and grassroot organizations fighting for the rights of undocumented immigrants. A handful of organizations have attacked the legal structure set against immigration by providing free legal services to undocumented immigrants. These organizations have been effective in overturning certain verdicts or changing local laws, specifically in progressive states like New York. Among the many organizations fighting for the rights of undocumented immigrants, United We Dream Action (UWDA) stands out as an example of a youth-led organization that promotes individual campaigns advocating at a local, state, or national level. UWDA takes grassroots forces and organizes them to facilitate justice and a voice for all. In past campaigns, they have succeeded in overturning legislation and spreading awareness. There are hundreds of such small organizations across the US—individually they are but a single voice, but together they yield tremendous power. Its effectiveness is difficult to quantify, as its tactics are not centered within the legal system but in the power of the masses to promote justice and affect change. It has, however, been able to prevent certain legislation and to create a nationwide platform from which to spread awareness.

Right now, to improve grassroots organizations' efforts to combat anti-immigrant advocates, I would argue that it is imperative that organizations like UWDA capitalize on the humanitarian issue arising from the current COVID-19 crisis. To build the massive movement necessary to affect change, one organization must take the lead to gather other organizations' support, at least initially. This could be UWDA. Building solidarity and commonalities between supporters of a movement is hugely unifying. COVID-19 has impacted every single person in the U.S., putting millions out of work but disproportionately targeting communities of color. Lacking a social security number, undocumented immigrants already cannot file for emergency provisions, such as unemployment compensation from the U.S. government. Additionally, the stimulus checks deemed necessary for pandemic emergencies by Congress are not distributed to undocumented immigrants (Koslof). Many are afraid to share their stories via the media, even anonymously, because of the obvious fear of deportation. Acting now, during COVID-19, and sharing these distressing stories might be our best chance at mobilizing the public's sympathy towards pushing for legislative change.

By mobilizing grassroots organizations to collect and publish stories and images of undocumented immigrants (in communities or in detention centers) during COVID and publicizing their plight via mainstream and social medias, the movement can use this crisis as a catalyst. It is also important to focus on publishing articles in historically progressive districts to speak to those already sympathetic to the cause. These articles must strongly advocate for the removal of the 1986 IRCA provision that requires a documentation check. Once people rally behind the cause, letter writing campaigns (advertised via organizations' mailing lists as well as in the media) will allow the movement to build until elected officials are no longer able to ignore it. Eventually, the removal of the undesirable IRCA provision could snowball into repealing other similarly destructive immigration laws.

To convince non-supporters, the grassroots movement should also point to how the current immigration law (IRCA) is duplicitous in trying to appear to uphold American values while actually undermining them. Embedded in the IRCA are provisions that "protect" *all* workers against abuse, discrimination, and wage discrimination. But the IRCA also prevents undocumented immigrants from working legally. It seems hypocritical to protect a worker who is not allowed to work in the first place. It's not too far of a stretch to convince the general public that there is only one clear solution to this contradiction—to remove the requirement that employers have to check immigration status when hiring—and make working a legal right for all.

We should also attempt to reach the sizable population who are anti-immigrant. For this, we need to convince them that what they are told is not necessarily true. Further down the line, the movement should publish "reverse conservative propaganda" articles. For example, telling trade unions that they could be stronger with the inclusion of the large and eager population of often abused undocumented workers.

Another tactic to garner public support is to encourage the public to identify with their nationalistic cause. In general, Americans who oppose immigration consider themselves highly patriotic. Hispanics constitute the largest minority in the U.S. military at 16%. Historically, untrusted racial groups have proven extremely patriotic, like the Japanese who were placed into internment camps in WWII. When asked to serve, many Japanese Americans left their internment camps to join the Army. They fought for the country that placed their families and loved ones in camps with barbed wire, becoming the most decorated Army unit in U.S. history. The message must be clear—Americans come from all over the world, and no one group has a monopoly on patriotism.

America is a nation of immigrants—only 2.6% of Americans are Indigenous People ("Indian Country Demographics"). Do we, as descendants of immigrants, have the right to terrorize any human for trying for a better life? If your immigrant great-grandfather had been deported for asking for a living wage, where would you be now? We must do more.

WORKS CITED

"Annual Report of Immigrant Visa Applicants in the Family-Sponsored and Employment-Based Preferences Registered at the National Visa Center as of November 1, 2019." U.S. Department of State, *Travel*, 1 Nov. 2019, https://travel.state.gov/content/dam/visas/Statistics/Immigrant-Statistics/WaitingList/WaitingListItem_2019.pdf.

Camarota, Steven. "Deportation vs. the Cost of Letting Illegal Immigrants Stay." *Center for Immigration Studies*, 3 Aug. 2017, https://cis.org/Report/Deportation-vs-Cost-Letting-Illegal-Immigrants-Stay.

Campbell, Monica. "For Undocumented Workers, Demanding Better Work Conditions Could Mean Deportation." *The World*, PRX, 26 Aug. 2019, https://www.pri.org/stories/2019-08-26/undocumented-workers-demanding-better-work-conditions-could-mean-deportation. Accessed January 11, 2021.

Courteau, Darcy. "Mireya's Third Crossing." *The Atlantic*, June 2019, https://www.theatlantic.com/magazine/archive/2019/06/border-crossings-one-immigrants-journey/588064/.

"COVID-19 Hospitalization and Death by Race/Ethnicity." *Centers for Disease Control and Prevention*, https://www.cdc.gov/coronavirus/2019-ncov/covid-data/investigations-discovery/hospital ization-death-by-race-ethnicity.html. Accessed January 10, 2021.

"ERO FY 2019 Achievements." *ICE*, Official Website of the Department of Homeland Security. https://www.ice.gov/features/ERO-2019#. Accessed January 13, 2021.

Gonzalez-Barrera, Ana and Jens Manuel Krogstad. "What We Know about Illegal Immigration from Mexico." *Pew Research Center*,28 June 2019, https://www.pewresearch.org/fact-tank/2019/06/28/what-we-know-about-illegal-immigration-from-mexico/. Accessed 31 May 2020.

Harris, Paul. "Undocumented Workers' Grim Reality: Speak Out on Abuse and Risk Deportation." *The Guardian*, 28 Mar. 2013, https://www.theguardian.com/world/2013/mar/28/undocumented-migrants-worker-abuse-deportation.

Hill, Travis Putnam. "Big Employers No Strangers to Benefits of Cheap, Illegal Labor." *The Texas Tribune*, December 19, 2016. https://www.texastribune.org/2016/12/19/big-name-businesses-exploit-immigrant-labor/.

"Immigration Rules: What Do Immigrants Need to Know about Unemployment Compensation?" *The Legal Aid Society of Cleveland*, https://lasclev.org/immigration-rules-what-do-immigrants-need-to-know-about-unemployment-compensation/. Accessed 9 Jan. 2021.

"Indian Country Demographics." *Demographics,* National Congress of American Indians, 1 June 2020, https://www.ncai.org/about-tribes/demographics.

"Japanese-American Service in World War II." *Wikipedia*. Wikimedia Foundation, January 5, 2021. https://en.wikipedia.org/wiki/Japanese-American_service_in_World_War_II.

Koslof, Evan. "VERIFY: No, the Stimulus Checks Won't Be Going to Undocumented Immigrants." *WUSA 9,* USA Today, 22Dec. 2020, https://www.wusa9.com/article/news/verify/verify-no-the-stimulus-checks-are-not-going-to-undocumented-immigrants-heres-where-the-confusion-started/65-70df43db-0145-492 d-a862-978640a2631f.

Lee, Michelle. "Analysis | Donald Trump's False Comments Connecting Mexican Immigrants and Crime." *The Washington Post,* WP Company, 15 Aug. 2018, https://www.washingtonpost.com/news/fact-checker/wp/2015/07/08/donald-trumps-false-comments-connecting-mexican-immigrants-and-crime/.

"Mexico–United States Border." *Wikipedia*, Wikimedia Foundation, 13 Jan. 2021, https://en.wikipedia.org/wiki/Mexico%E2%80%93United_States_border.

"Migrant Deaths along the Mexico–United States Border." *Wikipedia*. Wikimedia Foundation, January 10, 2021. https://en.wikipedia.org/wiki/Migrant_deaths_along_the_Mexico%E2%80%93United_States_border#cite_note-3.

"Most Mexicans See Better Life in U.S. - One-In-Three Would Migrate." Pew Research Center's Global Attitudes Project. Pew Research Center, May 31, 2020. https://www.pewresearch.org/global/2009/09/23/most-mexicans-see-better-life-in-us-one-in-three-would-migrate/.

Nowrasteh, Alex. "21 People Died in Immigration Detention in 2020." *CATO at Liberty*, CATO Institute, 22 Oct. 2020, https://www.cato.org/blog/21-people-died-immigration-detention-2020. Accessed 15 Jan. 2021.

Panetta, Grace. "Conservative Media Described Immigration as an Invasion' Hundreds of Times Before the El Paso Shooter Echoed the Same Language." *Business Insider*, 12 Aug. 2019, https://www.businessinsider.com/conservative-media-often-called-immigration-invasion-before-el-paso-2019-8. Accessed 15 Jan. 2021.

"Real ID Act." *Wikipedia*. Wikimedia Foundation, 14 Jan 2021, https://en.wikipedia.org/wiki/Real_ID_Act#National_ID_card_controversy.

Rodriguez, Adrianna. "Latinos Are Fastest Growing Population in US Military, but Higher Ranks Remain out of Reach." *USA Today,* Gannett Satellite Information Network, 11 June 2020, https://www.usatoday.com/in-depth/news/nation/2020/05/23/latino-hispanic-military-high-ranking-commissioned-officer-positions/4668013002/.

"Undocumented Workers." *Workplace Fairness,* https://www.workplacefairness.org/undocumented-workers#3.Accessed 11 Jan. 2021.

United States Border Control. "Southwest Border Sectors: To
tal Illegal Alien Apprehensions by Fiscal Year." *U.S. Bor
der Control*, https://www.cbp.gov/sites/default/files/as
sets/documents/2020-Jan/U.S.%20Border%20Patrol%20
Fiscal%20Year%20Southwest%20Border%20Sector%20Ap
prehensions%20%28FY%201960%20-%20FY%202019%29_0.
pdf

"When Breaking the Law by Hiring Illegal Aliens Doesn't Pay."
FAIR, Federation for American Immigration Reform,
November 2008, https://www.fairus.org/issue/societal-im
pact/when-breaking-law-hiring-illegal-aliens-doesnt-pay?g
clid=Cj0KCQiA6Or_BRC_ARIsAPzuer86VTVA2R7U
WyRuv3zfZ_ZreumztsescwqFlfy4U2UJ_9cMqeLccfoaApe
tEALw_wcB. Accessed 11 Jan. 2021.

*Emily Gaw is a rising sophomore at the University of Virginia, plan-
ning on majoring in Commerce. She is the only child of two immigrants. Her father is Thai; her mom is Irish. In her free time, she enjoys
skiing, photography, working on entrepreneurial projects, and spending time with friends and family.*

CHAPTER THIRTEEN

American Individualism

John Morgan

"You love what you take care of."

A few months ago, I was reading an opinion piece in the *New York Times* and this line, a quote from an unremembered source, framed the concluding point. The article detailed the author Anton DiSclafani attempting to campaign for the incumbent Doug Jones against his conservative challenger Tommy Tuberville. Although she knew that Jones would almost definitely lose, she continued to work for Jones because she viewed politics as an act of love. Most of the people of her state were against every political belief she held, but she wanted to care for them nonetheless. Even as the specifics of her piece dimmed in my mind, as evident by my need to reread the article to remind myself of who exactly DiSclafani was supporting, that quote held onto me: you love what you take care of.

I found this idea inspiring, that the same love I could express in my interpersonal relationships could extend towards caring for broader social movements. 2020 provided me with plenty of examples of just how powerful this could be. Protesters marching for Black Lives Matter, the unprecedented voter turnout in the recent election, and even wearing a mask to prevent the transmission of a virus all spread out before me, a mosaic of activism all connected by the central idea of care being an expression of love. It was beautiful. But, for every aspect of society where I found politics to be an act of love, I saw people walking in the opposite direction. Conflicting images arose and fractured the concept that I originally sought out; sure, there was plenty of care being given, but wasn't the opposite also true? People created movements to combat Black Lives Matter, perpetuating systems that favor themselves despite actively harming others; there was widespread support for intensely capitalistic institutions and policies that emphasize providing for oneself rather than entire communities; and people were choosing to disregard measures to combat COVID-19 which were designed to protect the entire country from the virus. Movements designed to help marginalized communities were championed by some but fought by others in the name of self-interest. I looked for examples of the quote I had read and explored the question of what Americans truly care about, what they truly love, but it stared back at me defiantly. I found myself asking what happens when care is misdirected; what happens when the love for oneself trumps the love we have for those around us?

Individuality and self-interest are a core part of American culture. There's an emphasis on achieving and providing for ourselves. We grow up being taught the "American Dream" in school, where if we would just work for what we want, anything is achievable. And the common protests against social programs (universal healthcare, for example) are rooted in the notion that people should be self-sufficient, not reliant on "handouts." None of this is to say that self-interest is inherently bad. We need to care about ourselves. However, when brought to extremes, self-interest can actively harm those around us. In the United States, hyper-individualistic tendencies have become ingrained within our culture, leading to a neglect of care towards those who need it most. Admittedly, when I began thinking about this issue, I was overwhelmed. It seemed too diffuse, so intangible— how could I begin to even think about this issue, much less try to think of its solutions? However, by taking an example of this hyper self-interest in action and by seeing all of the ills it has precipitated, I believe that the concept is much easier to tackle. As thousands of people die daily from the current pandemic, we can use how the United States has handled COVID-19 as a representation of how dangerous rampant self-interest can be.

The global pandemic plunged the entire world into a perpetual state of struggle. As both countries and individuals have been flung into a dark ocean of worry, with waves upon waves of new cases and deaths pummeling us as we struggle to keep our heads above water, the United States has drowned. According to the World Health Organization, as of 2020, the U.S. is the country with both the highest number of confirmed cases of COVID-19 *and* deaths due to it. There are two reasons why a pandemic is the perfect situation to highlight the effects of hyper self-interest in America: every country is confronted by the same issue synchronously and the social nature of the virus. During a pandemic, individuals are constantly asked to perform actions not for themselves, but for those who need care the most in society (the elderly, those with preexisting conditions, etc.). Wearing a mask, quarantining, and social distancing all require conscious efforts put forth by us as individuals in order to help the surrounding community. While many have adopted these practices, there are still many who haven't. Somehow, acts like wearing a mask are commonly viewed as a restriction of personal liberties rather than an act of care for those around them.

In many countries within East Asia, mask wearing is viewed in a different light, and their ardent use of masks is widely agreed to have helped them curb the spread of the virus. When interviewed about the difference between masking culture between the United States and other countries, Andrew Sieg, an engineer who has lived in both the U.S. and China, explained, "In East Asia, you are to wear a mask if you show any symptoms of being sick. This comes back to one culture valuing the well-being of society over the well-being of the individual." Even in Japan, which was criticized at the beginning of the pandemic for their lackadaisical response, cases are far lower than in the U.S. due to a culture of masking that has existed there even before COVID-19 was a threat. The United States may have a population approximately 2.5 times larger than Japan, but Japan has only had around 280 thousand confirmed cases while the U.S. has had nearly 23 million. Although the U.S. has over 80 times more cases than Japan, studies show that we are still less likely to wear masks in public. At the beginning of the pandemic, the low masking rates within the United States could be explained away by conflicting information coming from the scientific community or a lack of supply. Now, the widespread consensus is that masking works, and most businesses even carry extra masks for customers who need them. Failure to adopt these practices is not a question of difficulty but an active choice to go against what science says is best for those around us. We see people putting their wants over what is best for those around them. Despite all of this, I do not think the United States is a lost cause. Just as we have cultivated a culture where many lean towards caring for oneself over the community, we can create a culture of community caring.

How, then, can we begin to create this shift away from our current hyper-individualistic culture? I believe the answer lies within the same self-interest that is stopping us from preventing the pandemic in the first place. In activism, self-interest is both a barrier and tool for change; although it may prevent some from taking steps to protect people, it is also the driving force for those who actively care for those around them. Self-interest has become too focused on personal issues within the United States but appeals towards it are necessary to slowly expand the scope of problems we care about as a community. In Barack Obama's first memoir *Dreams From My Father*, a large portion is dedicated to him utilizing self-interest to garner support for his efforts to help communities within Chicago. He details how complicated the idea of self-interest truly is, saying, "The self-interest I was supposed to be looking for extended well beyond the immediacy of issues, that beneath the small talk and sketchy biographies and received opinions, people carried with them some central explanation of themselves. Stories full of terror and wonder, studded with events that still haunted or inspired them. Sacred stories." The notion of self-interest is far deeper than questions of someone's wants and opinions because people's senses of "self" cannot be explained so easily. People's senses of self also include their family, friends, coworkers, and the parts of their personal history which have forged the current way they view the world. Many aspects of people's hyper-individualistic tendencies are due to how the American identity is constructed through education and media; shifting the narrative away from this reliance on the capitalistic self-reliance inherent in the American Dream will take broad changes in the way we think about ourselves and our country. However, small-scale steps can be taken to influence people even within the United States' individualistic culture. By framing the movements in light of the external influences on people's identities, on the people and events that make up their senses of self, we can slowly build a culture of caring for others.

A powerful example of this is the efforts of Harvey Milk, one of the first openly gay elected officials in the United States, to convince people to come out. Milk knew the gay community needed broader support to get legislation passed, and he understood general appeals to those outside the community wouldn't cause them to actively support their cause. Knowing that people and their self-interests do not exist in a vacuum, Milk argues, "You must tell your relatives. You must tell your friends, if indeed they are your friends. You must tell your neighbors. You must tell the people you work with. You must tell the people in the stores you shop in. Once they realize that we are indeed their children, that we are indeed everywhere, every myth, every lie, every innuendo will be destroyed once and for all." Most Americans would not support something that doesn't directly affect them, but everyone's self-interests include other people as well. Instead of trying to combat people's individualistic nature by turning them towards a national issue, Milk used the pillars of people's sense of self to make a broad issue deeply personal. These people are still acting in self-interest, but now their interests are directed towards supporting a larger cause.

Self-interest can be used as a tool to expand people's circles, to make them care about more people, and as more Americans begin to care for those in their immediate interests, the more momentum there is towards changing the culture of individualism on a broader scale. The more groups and issues that we can integrate into our senses of self, the better we can care about them. It is difficult to grasp the full scale of a global pandemic, especially when it may not affect us directly, but by shifting the focus to protecting friends and family, we convince others to care about the larger issue. People's self-interests reach further than the immediacy of the issues they are personally confronting, and the more activists can tap into this, the more they can convince people to engage with broader issues within the country.

Although the pandemic exacerbated this issue, the problems that hyper-individualism can cause will not go away once it ends. Whether it's a movement like *BLM*, *#MeToo*, or an issue faced by any other marginalized group, having the support and care of those who are not facing those same difficulties is necessary. COVID-19 provides an example of the need to shift to a community-based mindset and an opportunity to integrate this mindset into other social movements. We love what we take care of, and there are so many people that need our love.

WORKS CITED

Obama, Barack. *Dreams from My Father: A Story of Race and Inheritance.* Canongate, 2016.

Capehart, Jonathan. "From Harvey Milk to 58 Percent." *The Washington Post*, WP Company, 22 Apr. 2019, www.washingtonpost.com/blogs/post-partisan/wp/2013/03/18/from-harvey-milk-to-58-percent/.

John (Jack) Morgan is a rising third year at the University of Virginia. He is double majoring in Biology and English and minoring in Philosophy. After growing up in Hudson, Ohio through high school, he now lives in Virginia full-time.

CHAPTER FOURTEEN

Dreams Without Bullets

Jolivette Mecenas

Over the past year, I began to keep a dream journal. While this might sound corny or childish for a nineteen-year-old college junior, I found the process comforting and often an amusing means of documenting the movements of my subconscious. One aspect of this practice which quickly became apparent, however, was the rate at which I ended dreams with a bullet in my brain. On a date, in school, or at the mall, faceless gunmen would spring from nowhere and with the squeeze of a trigger, I was dead. Terrifying and disturbing as these dreams are, I doubt I am alone in harboring this subliminal fear. Not only have all the innocuous locations of my dreams witnessed the effects of gun violence in the real world, but people my age have been bombarded with news of shootings since we were young. From Columbine to Virginia Tech Sandy Hook Elementary to the Emanuel African Methodist Episcopal Church, the Pulse nightclub in Orlando to the Las Vegas music festival and Marjory Stoneman Douglas High, mass shootings and their devastating effects have become a far too frequent feature of life in America.

Indeed, gun ownership in the United States is frighteningly banal. To highlight just how widespread gun possession in America is, Adam Lankford writes "Americans make up about 4.4 percent of the global population but own 42 percent of the world's guns" ("How American Gun Deaths"). According to the Center for Disease Control, in 2018 *alone* there were 39,740 deaths caused by firearms ("FastStats - Injuries"). Guns were the leading cause of both homicide and suicide from 1999 to 2016, contributing to 67.7% of homicides and 51.8% of suicides ("Should More Gun Control "). In addition, as documented by the Associated Press, in the 41 mass killings and resulting 211 deaths in the US in 2019, guns contributed to 33 of the incidents ("US Saw Highest Number"). Furthermore, in a study based on data from the National Violent Death Reporting System, there are an estimated 431 accidental deaths attributed to guns annually (Solnick). These stunning numbers, in conjunction with the horrifying tales relayed by news networks about the gun violence which occurs every day, paint a terrifying and tragically accurate portrait of American life. Not only do statistics show that gun violence is real, but in polls conducted by organizations such as Reuters and Ipsos, it was demonstrated that 59% of Americans fear random acts of gun violence as the greatest threat to their safety (Chan). And perhaps most tellingly, as stated by the American Journal of Medicine, "People in the U.S. are 25 times more likely to die from gun homicide than people in other wealthy countries" ("How American Gun Deaths"). Each of the aforementioned statistics demonstrate just how deeply gun possession and its innumerable consequences have percolated into the lives and consciousnesses of the American people.

These statistics should not remain the portrait of our country. Among the slew of problems we face every day, the thought that one might be gunned down without warning should not be so prevalent a stressor or so likely a possibility. However, the only means by which we can prevent such tragedies from remaining commonplace is through legislative efforts to reasonably restrict firearm purchases. In 2020, over 19 thousand people died in gun related incidents (Garcia-Navarro). Combined with the approximately 110,000 individuals who purchased guns in 2020 (47,000 of whom were first-time owners), it is clear that the firearm industry of the United States is thriving (Hubbard). Thus, unless more measures for controlling firearm purchases are taken, gun violence and gun-related deaths will continue to rise.

The question is what should be done? What can be done?

To begin an analysis of any topic as abidingly divisive as the issue of gun control, it is useful to consider history. As stated in the Constitution, "A well-regulated Militia, being necessary to the security of a free State, the right of the people to keep and bear Arms, shall not be infringed" ("The Second Amendment"). Though the phrasing and exact stipulations of the second amendment have long been debated, one fact cannot be argued is the right to possess arms is so fundamental to the United States that it was written into its most fundamental national document. As such, people often have strong and long-standing views in regard to gun ownership in United States. Proponents of their second amendment rights—Republicans, organizations like the NRA, and owners of guns or gun shops—are some of those who would most likely oppose legislation restricting gun rights. On the other side of the debate, families of the victims of gun violence, Democrats, and younger people like myself who have grown up in a climate where shootings are common are more likely to support measures for gun control. My goal in offering my vision for a safer America as well as the means by which we might achieve that vision is not to alienate, stereotype, or offend. As must be noted, I am no expert. However, as a humanist and fledgling advocate, my feelings and suggestions about the matter stem from a firm and committed belief in how we might provide future generations with a more secure and stable country.

My proposals for restrictions on gun purchases and ownership are not so overarching nor aggressive as some which have failed. I suspect that many of these failures can be attributed to the fear that these measures seek to reduce American freedoms by preventing all citizens from purchasing or owning guns of any sort, for any purpose. This is not my aim. Although I personally do not desire to purchase or own a gun, I respect those who do in pursuit of sport or self-defense. I furthermore support that it is the right of these people to own firearms, as this right was an important enough liberty to be outlined in the Constitution. However, despite the presence of the right to firearm possession at the national level, the rules for purchasing firearms themselves vary from state to state. Major requirements, according to the federal 1968 Gun Control Act, include purchasers be at least 18, have no felony convictions or involuntary commitments to mental institutions, possess a Federal Firearms License (FFL), and, in some states, undergo a background check based on the FBI's National Instant Criminal Background Check System (NICS). A notable exception to these requirements is the "gun show loophole" which enables people to obtain guns without FFLs or background checks provided they are sold from home, online, at flea markets, or gun shows, and the sale is not part of standard business activity (Welle).

At the time of the drafting of the Constitution, guns were not the efficient or effective weapons they have become today. The most common firearms of the 1790s were muskets and flintlock pistols, which in the hands of an expert wielder could fire a maximum of three rounds per minute with an accuracy range of about 50 meters. Today's armaments, such as the AR-15, can fire 45 rounds per minute at an accuracy range of 550 meters (Souerbry). A gun is not a tool as simple as a hammer or even a knife. Guns are weapons which necessitate expertise and careful usage. In other words, they are dangerous in the same sense in which a boat, plane, or even car is dangerous. Thus, it seems logical that much like a boat, plane, or car, the qualifications for purchasing and owning a gun should be similar to the qualifications for purchasing or owning one of these vehicles. However, in contrast to the aforementioned modes of transport, guns must be managed at a federal level, not to be impinged on or circumvented by the agendas of certain states or sellers. If arms are an uncompromised federal right, they deserve uncompromising federal regulations.

To this end, we must eradicate the gun show loophole. Following this, a person who would like to own a firearm should be subject to a test of proficiency with the weapon and made to obtain a specialized license based on the type of firearm desired. I understand the much-cited argument that many who oppose gun control legislation reference, about the right to own semi-automatic weapons, and I furthermore understand that the average person does not actually comprehend the capabilities of these weapons. However, I think there ought to be a different kind of license and test conducted to obtain different classes of weapons. Someone who can drive a car is not someone who can automatically handle a 72-foot semi-truck. The same holds true for someone who knows how to operate a double barrel shotgun versus someone who knows how to operate an AR-15 assault rifle.

As a feature of the licensing process, one must pass a universal background check, irrespective of the state one resides in, including a review of internet search history and social media profiles as well as a basic psychiatric test. The strongest argument against such checks remains the incursion into privacy. However, to counter this argument, I would remind those opposed that similar checks are compulsory for anyone entering most levels of the private and public sectors as well as the military, and thus these are not unprecedented or violative obligations.

I further suggest that those wishing to purchase firearms be made to carry liability insurance on the weapons. This way, gun holders will be incentivized to responsibly store their weapons, reducing accidental deaths and mitigating theft, an incredibly pervasive problem as shown by the 1.4 million guns which were stolen from US homes between 2005 and 2010 ("More Gun Control Laws?"). Finally, guns are significant pieces of property. And just like other important pieces of property such as houses and automobiles, they ought to be subject to taxes. Such taxes will generate revenue which can be used to reduce gun crime and its effects through education, victim compensation funds, and task forces to recover illegal weapons, much like gas taxes are used to fund road construction.

Although many of these efforts may seem ambitious, I truly think they are logical steps that can be taken for the betterment of our society. Gun shop owners may face a decrease in profits initially, but they will gain more respectability as gun ownership itself becomes more respectable and the stigmas around arms and those who bear them lose traction. Lethal conflicts will decrease, and horrifying incidents of police brutality will decrease with them, as more people might be willing to become officers if the likelihood of being killed in service decreases, thus allowing better candidates to be selected and overt racists like Derek Chauvin to be fired or never hired in the first place. Finally, safety in America will not be so questionable. Students will not worry about dying in class; club and concert goers will not dread being murdered mid-dance; and worshippers will not fear being killed for their race or religion.

I hope one day to dream unperturbed and be proud of the country in which I live. As Quinnipiac Poll notes, we are already headed in the right direction, given that "97% of American voters and 97% of gun owners support universal background checks" ("More Gun Control Laws?"). The next steps can be small. Petitions, protests, even efforts for the reduction of gun-glorifying media. Crucially, we must not allow this issue to slip offstage and languish on the pages of policymaker back catalogue until the next massacre occurs, as we have time and time again. We must take these steps now. We must make these efforts continuously. For if we do not, our country shall remain divided, disaster-filled, and deadly.

WORKS CITED

Chan, Melissa. "How Likely Is the Risk of Being Shot in America? It Depends." *Time*, 19 Aug. 2019, time.com/5476998/risk-of-guns-america/.

"FastStats - Injuries." Centers for Disease Control and Prevention, 13 Nov. 2020, www.cdc.gov/nchs/fastats/injury.htm.

Garcia-Navarro, Lulu, and Sonali Rajan. "2020 Was A Record-Breaking Year For Gun-Related Deaths In The U.S." *NPR*, 3 Jan. 2021, www.npr.rg/2021/01/03/952969760/2020-was-a-record-breaking-year-for-gun-related-deaths-in-the-u-s#:~:text=According%20to%20the%20Gun%20Violence,to%20gun%20violence%20in%202020.

"How American Gun Deaths and Gun Laws Compare to Canada's." *National Observer*, 4 Dec. 2015, www.nationalobserver.com/2015/12/04/news/how-american-gun-deaths-and-gun-laws-compare-canadas. Accessed 4 Dec. 2015.

Hubbard, Kaia. "California Firearm Purchases, Concerns of Violence Are Up During COVID-19 Pandemic." *U.S. News & World Report*, 19 Oct. 2020, www.usnews.com/news/best-states/articles/2020-10-19/california-firearm-purchases-concerns-of-violence-are-up-during-pandemic.

"Should More Gun Control Laws be Enacted?" *Gun Control*, Britannica ProCon.Org, 7 Aug. 2020, gun-control.procon.org/.

Solnick, Sara J. and David Hemenway. "Unintentional Firearm Deaths in the United States 2005–2015." *Injury Epidemiology*, BioMed Central, vol. 6, no. 42, 2019, https://doi.org/10.1186/s40621-019-0220-0

Souerbry, Rachel. "Here's What Firearms Looked Like When The Founding Fathers Wrote The Second Amendment." *Weird History*, Ranker, 9 Aug. 2019, www.ranker.com/list/firearms-in-1791/rachel-souerbry.

"The 2nd Amendment of the U.S. Constitution." *National Constitu tion Center* constitutioncenter.org/interactive-constitution/ amendment/amendment-ii.

"US Saw Highest Number of Mass Killings on Record in 2019, Data base Reveals." *BBC News*, BBC, 29 Dec. 2019, www.bbc. com/news/world-us-canada-50936575.

Welle, Deutsche. "8 Facts about Gun Control in the US: DW: 20.01.2020." DW, 20 Jan. 2020, www.dw.com/en/8-facts-about-gun-control-in-the-us/a-40816418#:~:text=The%20 Gun%20Control%20Act%20of,to%20people%2021%20 and%20older.

Emily Campbell (she/her) is a nineteen-year-old junior at the Univer-sity of Virginia currently pursuing English and Anthropology majors and a Psychology minor. After college, she hopes to exercise her lifelong passions for reading, writing, and discussion in a field where she may actively work to help others.

CHAPTER FIFTEEN

My First Time Standing Up For What I Believe In

Dorienne Hochard

These are a few photographs I took during the Women's March on October 17, 2020. I found that many of the fundamental principles of democracy played out on that day. For the first time, I got to witness people, many of whom were my age, passionately speaking up about what they believe. I found it inspiring that they were able to articulate their messages in such a persuasive manner. I was glad that I had the opportunity to listen. The march was quickly organized a week prior by leaders of the Women's March because Supreme Court Justice Ruth Bader Ginsburg had recently passed away. Despite her last wishes, the existing administration decided to push forward and fill her seat on the Supreme Court a few weeks prior to the upcoming election. I was devastated by her passing, and I felt like these actions were disrespectful to her life and career. She fought hard to stand up for what she believed was right, and I decided that I needed to follow the precedent that she set. Organizers of the Women's March sprung to action to mobilize voter outreach prior to the election by emphasizing the situation surrounding the new Supreme Court appointee and other current events affecting women that were going on at the time. This timing was crucial to illustrate the high stakes of the upcoming election to women, and it worked: women voters turned out at higher rates than they did in the presidential election of 2016. It was moving to be a part of this cause.

That morning I woke up almost giddy; I came home from college to specifically meet my friend in Washington, D.C. to attend the march. I was 19-years-old, and this was my first time getting physically involved and going out to protest. It changed my entire point of view; it changed my life. People of all ages gathered in Freedom Plaza; we listened to several speakers before commencing our march. I found the entire experience to be very empowering, I felt like I was a part of a cause larger than myself; in particular, one of the speakers was 15-years-old. While I cannot remember her name, I will never forget the scene of her standing tall at the podium giving her speech. Her mother had spoken to the crowd earlier, and she was right there while her daughter was speaking; she was even mouthing along to some of her daughter's speech as she read it to the crowd. You could see in her body language how proud she was of her daughter. I could not even imagine being 15-years-old and getting up to speak in front of thousands of people at once. It must have taken so much courage to go up there and deliver such a powerful speech about her Indigenous sisters, brothers, and ancestors. This whole scene only drew me in further and made me more inclined to listen to what *all* of the speakers had to say.

While everyone had their own motivations or reasons to join the march, it provided an opportunity for discussion and for different perspectives to be heard. I was there for a multitude of reasons. I was there to support women. I was there to proudly state that Black lives matter. I was there to support those who are a part of the LGBTQIA+ community. I was there and socially distanced to demonstrate that science is real. Most importantly, I was there to uphold my belief that *everyone* should be treated equally and justly under the law. Once I got to interact with others there, it sparked this sense of unity I had never quite felt before; there is something about marching through the streets of Washington that physically makes you feel as if your demands are being heard. It was a public declaration of what we demanded from our government. This was the true demonstration of fighting for the needs of the American people by being physically present to speak our minds.

The next morning, I woke up and found a picture of my buddy and I from the march in the *Washington Post*. It was a surreal feeling and a way of capturing and solidifying the memory of my first march.

Usually I read the articles and look through the photos, but this is the time where I decided to become a part of them and the movement for a better future for all.

Dorienne Hochard is a second-year student at the University of Virginia where she is double-majoring in Chemistry and Global Studies: Middle East & South Asia. She's been inspired by her peers taking action in emerging social issues; she will stand up to amplify their voices because everyone deserves to be heard.

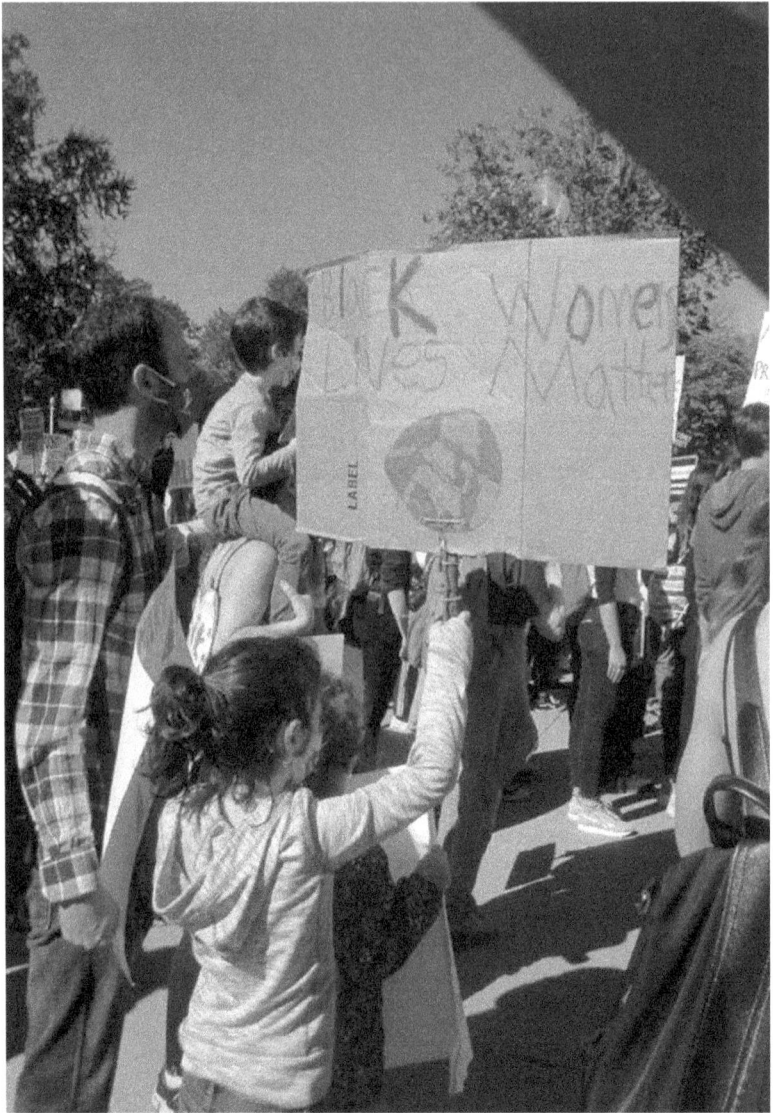

CHAPTER SIXTEEN

Nicaragua

Iris Jung

During my sophomore year of high school in 2018, my peers and I encountered the Nicaraguan protests that defined many of our lives. In the lackluster country I had called home, this sudden explosion of violence forced me to stop and witness a new reality. At first, like many of my peers, I was determined to bring a change. I held banners in my hands and shouted for human rights and democracy. My friend and I created a community for those who felt a similar passion, encouraging ongoing private and public gatherings. Looking at those who had joined together to fight for what was considered right, a surge of dedication and resolve enveloped us all. We were not alone. I could see a new future beginning to form with each passing day. This wave overwhelmed the city of Managua within a single week. I found myself in the midst of strangers gathered around a common purpose. After years of silent endurance, I watched and participated as the people of Nicaragua demanded for change.

By the second week, there were no remains of the protests that had swept through the country. Instead, militias lined the streets as masked groups fought back with makeshift guns and spray paint. Walking through the streets, the portraits and names of the disappeared consumed the walls. Although so many had been forced into silence, some continued to push back and call for justice. However, unlike the start of the protest, the efforts grew more futile with each passing day. Not only were the few who continued to protest disappearing, but President Ortega had planted distrust in the people of Nicaragua with his Sandinista party. In the middle of summer that year, the piercing sounds of gunshots struck the air as the National Police massacred hundreds at the University of Nicaragua. That day I could only hold my friend in my arms as she wept for her brother, who only hoped to bring about a brighter future for his country.

The Nicaraguan protests were not new events within the country of Nicaragua. The initial protests began in 2014, following the construction of the Nicaragua Canal. Not only did this lead to Ortega's implication in a corrupt electoral system, but it also planted tremendous distrust within civilians against their government. In the spring of 2018, these protests roared to life once again with the news of social security reforms. Ortega and his family's attempt at these reforms, according to prominent rumors, was a consequence of their lavish spendings and abandonment of their people. Despite the lack of monetary funds being blatantly the fault of the Ortega administration, which included his family, those who would bear the ramifications would be the people of Nicaragua. After the initial protests and their violent responses, Ortega quickly retracted his statement on the reforms. However, the horrific attacks and inhuman acts of brutality were fresh in the minds of family members, friends, and loved ones. The purpose of the demonstrations changed. During those moments, the issue of international human rights became the burning issue I committed to.

Human rights are a set of rights and freedoms every individual obtains without discrimination. These rights are based on the values of dignity, fairness, equality, respect and independence.[1] These values are ones that I hold with personal importance. My vision for human rights is expressed in the Declaration, which states, universal human rights are one that create the basis for freedom, justice, and peace. These three foundational rights are ones I also associate with democracy. Therefore, I believe these rights should be the foundation for every individual's life. However, in my country, I would argue that the specific rights to the freedom of speech, freedom of thought, and freedom from fear are the highest priority. After my experience in Nicaragua, I witnessed that these three freedoms were imperative for both the people and oppressors. This was due to the freedoms' ability

---

1. "What Are Human Rights?" equalityhumanrights.com. Equality and Human Rights Commission, 19 June 2019, https://www.equalityhumanrights.com/en/human-rights/what-are-human-rights.

to create dignity, worth, and improvement in the living standards of an individual (ex. life without fear). As a result, my vision for the future of human rights has the three freedoms of speech, thought, and fear as its basis. I am certain, with the restructuring of these human rights by pulling against the pillars of the Ortega regime, that Nicaragua will find itself in the light of a new future.

In the country of Nicaragua, these three basic human rights were violated after the 2018 Nicaraguan Protests, which were a result of Ortega's blatant injustice towards Nicaraguans. Despite the anti-government protests maintaining peaceful assembly, they were met with brutality and violence. By April 2018, 328 individuals had been killed and over 2,000 were injured. In addition, over 700 protesters were imprisoned and tortured, leading to a wave of fear throughout the country.[2] Human rights defenders, those who spoke out against the violations by the government, also became the targets of threats, harassment, and unjust arrests. Despite having low public support, the power of Ortega and his Sandinista party seemed endless. Like most governments, Nicaragua's government maintains its power through their Pillars of Support, the institutions and publics (such as education or the media) through which hegemonic power is maintained. Out of the numerous pillars, the three I identify as most crucial to Ortega maintaining his power are the security forces, the commercial/business institution, and the international community. With the correct strategy, these pillars can also lead to his collapse.

Security forces: In Nicaragua, there are two main forces that maintain Ortega's regime: the National Police and armed Sandinista organizations. These groups play a central role in the physical oppression of the people and initiate fear throughout the country. More importantly, they create a fear of sanctions, one of the real sources of political power. This can be most clearly seen with the Sandinista's use of undercover agents to root out and physically harm those demonstrating against the regime. Certain houses would be marked with red to indicate the violence that would fall upon the house. Within a week, these houses would be burned to the ground, regardless of the human beings that were inside. In addition, the National Police would line every corner of the city, tensely prepared for any sign of demon-

---

2. "Nicaragua." *heritage.org*. The Heritage Foundation, n.d., https://www.heritage.org/index/country/nicaragua. Accessed 10 January 2021.

stration. Even the slightest of gatherings would provoke terrifying attacks and mass arrests. Those who were arrested failed to return or return home in a battered state. One of my peers lost her brother, who simply never returned home, in this manner. However, in response to these acts, when protestors countered with similar means as these security forces, the brutality only increased, which I had thought impossible. Thus, nonviolent movements are imperative in combating these security forces. Due to the ruthless actions of individuals on both sides, there is an animosity that promotes increasing violence and hatred. Therefore, through nonviolent movements, this animosity can decrease, encourage pro-government officials against callous treatment, and sway these individuals. In addition, the use of dispersion tactics will prevent police and armed individuals from excessive violence. As a result, even if these groups refuse to join anti-government movements, the brutality of their actions will lessen.

Commercial institutions: Due to the authoritarian government led by Ortega, the economy of Nicaragua has declined. This, according to the *Heritage Foundation*, has only been accelerated as a consequence of the political crisis in the country. Further, economic tensions have increased after the European Union's asset freeze of top Nicaraguan officials. With the lack of economic support from major powers, as a third world country, Nicaragua faced increased financial difficulty. For example, the price of eggs or milk increased five times its original price. However, major institutions within Nicaragua were quickly dominated by the regime, allowing a select few access to basic needs. However, there is no doubt that these institutions would continue to require customers outside of those belonging to the regime. To gain the support of the commercial or economic institutions, the people of Nicaragua could mobilize through non-cooperation tactics. Not only would this be low-risk and encourage participation, but it would also have a significant impact on the economy and invite these institutions to support anti-government movements. If institutions that have supported Ortega are boycotted in a quiet and discreet manner, not only would they suffer financial crisis, but it would be a silent victory for those continuously fighting against Ortega's regime.

International community: Without a doubt, the actions taken in Nicaragua can be seen as ethically incorrect and violations of human rights. From the government's complete control of freedoms to the vicious murder of citizens, it is obvious something must be done. Despite this blatant fact, there has been little change in Nicaragua. Although the wrongdoings of the Nicaraguan officials have been brought to attention, the international community has failed to maintain pressure on the country, allowing oppression to continue. As a result, more than 88,000 Nicaraguans have been forced to abandon their homes and seek asylum wherever they can.[3] Although international communities (Human Rights Watch; United Nations) must be responsible in upholding universal human rights and enforcing consequences, the people of Nicaragua can also take action. This action can be taken through public acts. This method would be nonviolent, but also garner the attention of the media, encouraging people throughout the world to take notice. For example, my peers and I have been continuously sharing the witness testimonies and experiences of those who remain in Nicaragua. Although our platforms are not large, many have taken note of Nicargua's reality and shared this news with others. As the truths of the Nicaraguan people continue to spread throughout the world, the pressure on Ortega and the international community will grow proportionally, forcing further action and prevention of inhuman acts of violence by Ortega and his regime.

As a witness to the brutality in 2018, I felt a realization and determination. Although I am a single individual, it became my goal to take action against this cruel and oppressive government. It was in this context I analyzed what pillars supported and could topple Ortega. And now, within that strategy, I intend to use my education, my writing, to amplify the voices of those who have been suppressed, through which I can uplift underrepresented individuals and communities. Through my writing, I hope to improve this skill to not only convey my motivations, but to also persuade and urge others to join the movement towards these goals. Further, I hope to use writing to encourage others to feel a similar sense of burning justice and take the action they can. I believe this is imperative because the goals and issues that plague the world today can only be solved through unity and alliance.

---

3. "Nicaragua." *hrw.org*. Humans Right Watch, n.d., https://www.hrw.org/world-report/2020/country-chapters/nicaragua.

Ultimately, however, the burning issue of international human rights is one that must be solved as a community, not just by individual actions. In addition to the people within these countries taking actions, those around the world must also take notice and encourage those protesting against their oppressors. For example, this can be done through the spread of information and news on social platforms. This will not only increase awareness and knowledge on these issues, but it will also create pressure on the international community and countries towards change. However, it is important that this pressure remains constant until change is applied to the countries facing difficulty. By taking action to apply international human rights to everyone, we can take steps towards creating a world with rights and freedoms for every individual. This will allow us, as a society, to view one another as valuable individuals. Finally and most importantly, these actions will allow us to achieve a greater dream of improving the world for those who come after.

Iris Y. Jung is an undergraduate student at the University of Virginia, pursuing a degree in Politics and English. Although Iris was born in Los Angeles, California, she has spent much of her childhood in Korea, Central America, and South America. After witnessing political events in Central and South American countries, Iris found her passion in politics. As a result, she hopes to pursue a career in international law in the future. ing professionals, college-age students, political activists, and fluffy.

CHAPTER SEVENTEEN

Jamaica Plain, a Day

Augustus Huang

8:00 AM. I settle into my chair and swivel forward, powering on the company laptop at my "desk"—a portable folding table that takes up minimal space. In this moment, the domain represents a working space. A nook in the apartment where I manipulate spreadsheets and join conference calls. But later in the day, it will be my leisure space. The ongoing pandemic has made it such that I've spent more of my professional career working out of a bedroom than out of an office building. My best navy-blue suit hangs in the closet nearby, flanked by sweatshirts and t-shirts that have gotten most of the attention as of late. Each day carries a sense of longing to see my colleagues in person again.

I turn to look outside the window of my third-story room. The neighboring building is within arm's reach, so there's not much of a view. I have clear sight of the balcony, and on it sit three children's' bicycles leaning against a worn wooden railing. The bicycles have been there since I settled here several months ago, and I have never seen anyone come to move them. The windows of that same neighboring building are boarded shut with cardboard-colored wood, so I wonder if anyone even lives there. Throughout the morning, the bicycles listen to my conversations and watch me tap away at the keyboard.

This is Jamaica Plain. And more than being a neighborhood in Boston, it is a rich experience. It is a defiant and proud microcosm that refuses to be neatly defined. An eclectic mish-mash of families, working professionals, college-age students, political activists, and fluffy cats, "JP" eschews cookie-cutter suburbia while declining the label "city." It is a world of contrasts and harmony. Yin and Yang.

1:00 PM. I finish lunch before grabbing a facemask to go for a midday walk around the block. I make my way out of the front door and take a deep breath of air. Clear and fresh this time, but in truth I never know for certain what I'm going to get. Sometimes the scent is meat grilling. Sometimes there is a heavy waft of cannabis. I hear excited chatter coming from the front steps of the Ana Luisa—a family-operated daycare across the street. I stand on Dalrymple Street, which to me encapsulates the elusive essence of JP that makes it so special. Apartment units line the road, standing at identical heights, each with three floors. At the same time, no two buildings possess the same color or style of siding. Like a quilt, the street exhibits close-knit unity while its parts express individuality.

The first local landmark I stroll past is the Samuel Adams Brewery. True to the quirky personality of the neighborhood it inhabits, the brewery complex dons crimson walls decorated with abstract murals of distorted faces and psychedelic patterns. A bronze statue of Mr. Adams juxtaposes these sights a few paces away. The courtyard is empty now—patiently waiting for the day ale-lovers and neighbors can come again and mingle under the soft golden glow of the patio string lights. In the meantime, the brewery continues to churn and distribute seasonal lagers across the country. Branded trucks line the lots, prepared for loading. A lot of domestic beer comes from this relatively small production hub nested cozily amongst residential homes.

Continuing through the neighborhood, I witness a young woman bringing a compost bin out to the curb for pickup. "Bootstrap Compost" buckets scatter the walkways, each filled with scraps that will soon be used to help carry on the cycle of cultivation. Further down the block, I observe the yard signs and posters that are creatively arranged on porches and driveways—in windows and gardens. Some of these signs loiter from last November, when denizens were actively pushing for referenda actions that were decided on Election Day. YES ON 2—RANKED CHOICE VOTING. Others remained as perennial fixtures of solidarity. Black Lives Matter.

6:00 PM. I rub my eyes and massage my temples after I send the last email of the day. I write down everything I need to work on the next day, lest I forget, and shut down the company laptop. I stand up to stretch and prepare to go outside again before dinner. With my sneakers laced, I set out and run up and down the Southwest Corridor Park, which is mostly just a straight path that runs parallel to the Orange Line railroad tracks used for public transit. Along the way, I spot high-schoolers playing basketball and listening to hip-hop just feet away from adults on park benches ooh-ing and ahh-ing at each other's dogs and infants. Explicit lyrics permeate the backdrop, but the toddlers bop and giggle with approval.

7:30 PM. I take out pasta and vegetables prepared from the weekend and toss them into a pan over the stove. With a bit of seasoning, the simple stir-fry tastes great. Hunger is the best spice. I sit at the dining table and eat quietly, at once fatigued and thankful for the opportunity to fare another day in these uncertain times. I hurriedly wash the dishes before retreating to my room which is now my leisure space. I sit down at the folding table and read for a bit, but soon change gears because tonight I have a project to work on—to reflect on what democracy means to me personally. I identify the emotions democracy evokes from within me, but nonetheless I find myself at a loss for eloquence when it comes time to write. I feel any words I could muster would not do these feelings justice.

8:30 PM. Out of habit I lean back and peer out the window. The bicycles still lean against the railing, just barely visible now under the moonlight. I ponder my surroundings for inspiration and close my eyes. I then think of how democracy works to remove thick lines between social classes, vocations, and backgrounds. I reflect on how democracy allows us to express our differences proudly while coming together as a community. I contemplate how democracy encourages us to act in support of our ideas and our posterity—including in times when we must muster all our strength in order to remain resilient. There is not always concord, but we do not tolerate hate.

I recall the days of warmer weather when I would stand in the Egleston Community Orchard a few blocks away and sniff the sweet aroma of the violet lilacs. Charmed by its variegated flora and its presence as a plot of greenspace squeezed between Jamaica Plain housing units, I went on to learn that the orchard was initiated and is fully maintained by neighbors year-round. Once a vacant lot, the orchard is now a public space dedicated to collaboration, gatherings, and the arts. Amidst the terror and violence that still ails communities across the country, the garden reminds me of our search for peace.

My mind then flashes back to a previous weekend when I participated in *Ride for Black Lives*, a community-organized bike ride around the city of Boston that was started in Jamaica Plain. During this ride, dozens of community members of all ethnicities and walks of life came out to take over the streets of Boston, calling out peaceful chants and making our unified voices heard by the many shoppers, diners, pedestrians, and drivers across Beantown. Some passersby voice their dissent, but most honk or cheer with excitement and support of our assorted group of cyclists on that sunny afternoon. We conclude at the lush greens of Boston Common with gratitude, speeches, and calls to action. With this in mind, a proper symbol to convey the spirit and nature of democracy becomes clear—and I smile to myself because I am proud of where I call home in this current moment.

At the top of my blank word processor, in letters centered, I type: "Jamaica Plain, a Day."

Augustus Huang is a Product Manager at Bank of America Merrill Lynch. He is passionate about creating better products and services for a firm that seeks to drive social change in surrounding communities. He is a 2019 graduate of the University of Virginia McIntire School of Commerce and enjoys using writing as a medium for self-expression and reflection. "Jamaica Plain, A Day" is an introspective account of Augustus's time living in Boston, MA during the COVID-19 pandemic.

AFTERWORD

Domenick Bailey

James Baldwin once famously wrote, "I love America more than any other country in the world, and, exactly for this reason, I insist on the right to criticize her perpetually." This sentiment, one of dissent, patriotism, accountability, love, and protest, is skillfully and powerfully embodied in the spirit of *The Lived Experience of Democracy: Criticizing Injustice, Building Community.* This anthology, largely written and edited by college students at the University of Virginia, reflects an accessible and democratic production and refinement of knowledge. The book itself is a moving marriage of the qualitative and the quantitative, featuring that which is borne out in research and that which is undeniable by personal experience.

This book bravely confronts the tension between assimilation and accommodation, conformity and comfort, and self and community. It takes a close look at American institutions, spanning the gamut of healthcare, immigration, education, and more. The work intimately inspects the aspects of democracy and community that are obvious or taken for granted, examining that which we should accept and that which we should challenge. Bringing to the forefront the voices and perspectives of passionate and informed young advocates, this book is transformative. The authors of this anthology serve as powerful illustrations of college students who must meet the demands of striving for academic excellence, while simultaneously taking up the mantle of moving their respective communities forward.

As such, this anthology represents a powerful advocacy for the marginalized and disenfranchised. Holistically, it is sociology, anthropology, political science, and more. A product of the personal and the political, the featured texts challenge the reader to imagine that which has been deemed unattainable or "too good to be true." This book reveals the crucial fact that a community does not build, let alone improve, itself. Featuring fresh, bold, and innovative solutions, everyone from the policymaker to the student would be wise to heed the lessons set forth in this book, in order to move closer to the equitable and inclusive communities we should all be striving for.

Domenick Bailey graduated with distinction from the University of Virginia in 2022 as an Echols Scholar double-majoring in Sociology and Psychology. During his time at UVA, Bailey conducted significant research in public policy, including co-authoring Race, Policing and Public Governance alongside Dr. Brian N. Williams. Additionally, Bailey worked as an Education Policy Associate where he collaborated with Dr. Jim Wyckoff to co-author a policy brief for the Virginia Department of Education on racial disparities within gifted education in the Commonwealth.

Bailey has been admitted to Harvard Law School and will be enrolling in the fall of 2024, where he plans to continue studying the convergence of law and public policy, with a specific interest in civil rights and anti-discrimination practices.

Contributors

Niharika:
Niharika is a second-year at UVA studying Math and Economics. Applying her love for problem-solving and nature, she hopes to tackle environmental sustainability throughout her career. As a second-generation immigrant from India, she's also interested in racial and economic inequality. She intends to work on these issues through journalism and volunteer work in both America and India. And finally, she wishes to see educational reform across the US so that students of all backgrounds and identities are able to find a safe space within which to express their true selves.

Angela:
Angela is a third year at the University of Virginia majoring in Leadership and Public Policy. She currently works as the Treasurer for Black Student Leaders in Policy, the Social Action Co-Chair for Undergraduate Black Student Law Association, and an intern for the New City Community Press Initiative. As a first generation immigrant from Ghana, she hopes to utilize her passion for social justice and equity in order to improve disparities in quality education access and food insecurity domestically and globally.

Kaitlyn:
Kaitlyn is a second-year at the University of Virginia studying history with a concentration in law and society. She has also pursued extensive coursework in political theory and composition studies. In her research, she has analyzed the ways in which women have interacted with the law even when denied civil status. She has also produced research on the application of feminist pedagogy in humanities classrooms. In her free time, she is active in pro-choice politics, serving as the Vice President of Planned Parenthood Generation Action on grounds. She is also a consent educator and a writing tutor. After college, she plans to take her passion for the promotion of women's rights to law school.

Keilah:
Keilah is a second year at the University of Virginia double majoring in African American and African studies and Political and Social Thought. While working as the director of strategy of BRIDGE (Bringing Race into Dialogue Through Group Engagement) they have worked with various groups at the University to question both systemic and individual acts of racism and the flagrant normalization of racist action at UVA. Stemming from her commitments to environmental justice in various organizations, they spend their free time exploring the connections –and hierarchies that perpetuate– anti-Blackness and anti-environmentalism. Following their undergraduate career at UVA, they wish to continue their academic career by studying the ways Blackness presents itself in the political world.

Elise:
Elise is a second year student at the University of Virginia studying Music and Speech Communication Disorders.She is heavily involved with the arts at UVA, [participating in University and Chamber Singers, New Dominions a cappella, and First-Year Players. She also serves as Deputy-Director of the Arts Agency under Student Council, where she works on advocating for equity and accessibility within the arts at UVA. She hopes to use her time at UVA to create more opportunities for students to engage with the arts, integrate them into the undergraduate experience, and find intersections between the arts and social issues, such as the ones highlighted in this book.

Hannah:
Hannah is a second-year student at the University of Virginia studying Global Sustainability and Economics. As the event coordinator for the UNA-USA Chapter at UVA, a Green Dining Sustainability intern, and a Zero Waste Ambassador, she advocates for clean energy initiatives and systemic waste minimization, especially through collaboration with local businesses owned by marginalized individuals. She also values advancing educational equity, which she does through tutoring ESL elementary school students as well as judging regional debate tournaments. Following her time at UVA, she seeks to promote intersectional environmentalism and sustainable development through both policy work and political activism.

Sophia:
Sophia is a second year student at the University of Virginia majoring in Neuroscience with a minor in East Asian studies. She is involved in organizations such as VISAS, which aims to bet-

ter connect international students with the community. She is passionate about overturning racial and social inequalities and stigma by fostering close, interpersonal relationships at the university, and hopes to continue this on a larger scale as well. After graduating from college, she plans to pursue a career in the medical field as a physician, but will continue to fight against inequalities in the healthcare system and find ways to speak up and change the flaws that disadvantage so many people health-wise in the US.

www.ingramcontent.com/pod-product-compliance
Lightning Source LLC
Chambersburg PA
CBHW031436270326
41930CB00007B/733